BRUCE MCARTHUR

THE TORONTO GAY VILLAGE MURDERS

KILLER QUEENS
BOOK FOUR

ALAN R. WARREN

Copyright © 2022 Alan R. Warren
All rights reserved.

All rights reserved. No part of this book may be reproduced, scanned, or distributed in any printed or electronic form without permission of the author. The unauthorized reproduction of a copyrighted work is illegal. Criminal copyright infringement, including infringement without monetary gain, is investigated by the FBI and is punishable by fines and federal imprisonment. Please do not participate in or encourage privacy of copyrighted materials in violation of the author's rights. Purchase only authorized editions.

House of Mystery Publishing

Seattle, Washington, USA

Vancouver, British Columbia, Canada

First Edition

ISBN (Paperback): 978-1-989980-71-2
ISBN (eBook): 978-1-989980-67-5

Cover design, formatting, layout, and editing by Evening Sky Publishing Services

CONTENTS

Preface v
Introduction xiii

PART I

1. Toronto Gay Village — 3
2. Bruce McArthur — 17
3. First Blood 2001 — 23

PART II

4. Skandaraj "Skanda" Navaratnam 2010 — 33
5. Abdulbasir "Basir" Faizi 2010 — 37
6. Majeed "Hamid" Kayhan 2012 — 43
7. Zambian Meat Website — 47
8. Project Houston 2012 — 55
9. Soroush Mahmudi 2015 — 63
10. Dean Lisowick 2016 — 67
11. Selim Esen April 2017 — 71
12. Andrew Kinsman June 2017 — 73
13. Bruce McArthur's Interrogation — 79
14. Project Prism July 2017 — 105
15. Kirushuna Kumar Kanagaratnam Sept. 2017 — 109

PART III

16. The Arrest of McArthur   115
17. Trial & Sentencing   123

PART IV

18. Gay Village Murders 1975-1978   129
19. Murder of Emanuel Jaques   149
20. More Murders in Gay Village 2017   153
21. Police Review   161
22. Survivors   169
23. Todd McArthur   177

Timeline of Events   181
References   187
About the Author   191
Also by Alan R. Warren   193

PREFACE

Killer Queens is a new series of historical fiction books based on true stories. Sources, such as police reports and newspaper articles, are examined to gather as many facts surrounding each case. As with any work of fiction, some creative additions were made when recounting these stories, usually in the conversations between the personalities involved. The various sources are the basis of these conversations and, hopefully, make them come alive for the readers to help understand what was meant by those words.

One of the most common questions in gay-related murders is: how are they different from heterosexual murders? This question is important, as homosexuality was considered a criminal act for so many years. The *Killer Queens* series of books explores the world of murder in the gay community, whether the victims or the killers themselves, and sometimes both, are homosexual.

If you were caught performing a homosexual act in the Victorian Era, they would say you were "sexually insane" and commit you to an insane asylum. By the early 1900s, most countries decided it was more of a deviant act, something you shouldn't do. They would put you in a regular prison instead of an insane asylum if caught. By doing so, homosexuality became a crime, not as severe as murder, but more on the level of crimes such as theft, burglary, or arson.

A stunning example of the treatment of homosexuals in society is that of Alan Turing. Turing was a British mathematician, cryptanalyst, and computer scientist during World War II. In 1939, he joined the Hut 8 team. There, he solved the German Enigma code, which was considered the turning point for the Allied Forces winning the war against the Nazis.

So, what did society decide to do with one of its heroes?

Alan Turing was a homosexual. In 1952, when he was 39 years old, he started a relationship with Arnold Murray, who was 19. Shortly after the couple began seeing each other, Turing's house was robbed. After the police investigated the crime, they discovered that the thief was Murray and that Turing and Murray had been acquainted. It was also found that the two men had been involved in a sexual relationship. Both men were charged with gross indecency. Turing later pleaded guilty to the charges and was convicted. He was given a choice between imprisonment or conditional probation. What were the conditions he had to meet?

Turing had to undergo physical and hormonal changes designed to reduce his libido. He received several injections over one year, which feminized his body. During that year, he became impotent and grew breast tissue. Along with his body changes, he had his security clearance removed and lost his job with the British Intelligence Agency. He tried to move to America, but they denied him as he was then a convicted felon.

On June 7, 1954, Turing committed suicide in his home by ingesting cyanide. His housekeeper found him with a half-eaten apple lying beside him in his bed the following day. It was hypothesized that he had doused the apple with the cyanide. An inquest later determined that he had committed suicide.

When society forces one of its citizens to be sterilized for being homosexual, one considered to be among the best and a war hero, why would they care about other homosexuals being murdered or hurt?

It didn't end there.

Even after homosexuality was legalized in 1967, it was still considered a sickness or illness in the medical community that needed curing. Almost like alcoholism, only the general public looked at alcoholics with sympathy. After all, they were still pleasing people, and it was just the alcohol that made them do bad things. It was the Christian thing to do to help them. Most alcoholics weren't even arrested for driving while drunk or starting a fight in a public place. They were merely told to go home and sleep it off; if they kept on fighting, they were put in the drunk tank by the police for a night.

Whereas, if you were having or attempting to have sex with someone of the same sex as yourself, you were a pervert. It was considered wrong, disgusting, dirty, and perverted behavior. It was also judged as something you didn't need to do.

Why would someone want to have sex with another of their same-sex?

The public didn't know what to do with homosexuals after they were no longer considered criminals or insane. At least with alcoholics and drug addicts, there were treatments for their problems; after all, they just needed not to do it!

So, what would they do when they couldn't arrest these homosexuals or put them into the local mental institute? History repeated itself, and they turned it over to the religion of the day to handle.

In the past, when "dealing with" the Indigenous people of North America, the church and state decided that to "civilize the savage," they had their children forcibly extracted from the reserves they were imprisoned on and taken to Catholic schools to learn how to be "good Christians." Only now, many years later, an astounding number of unmarked graves are being discovered all over Canada, where Indigenous children were buried after their deaths at these residential schools. We do not even know the names of these children or why or how they died. Despite this atrocity, they believed they were successful in those cases with people they didn't understand, and they figured they would be successful in handling the gay population with the same iron fist.

So, keeping up with societal tradition, Evangelicals developed a new program to cure homosexuals. It was called "Exodus." In other words, they intended to "Pray away the Gay." They convinced several young gay men and women that the devil's influence made them believe they were gay and could fix their "problem" if they turned their lives over to the Lord and worked through the Exodus program. If they did, they would be cured, but they would be able to live healthy, productive, straight lives. As with so many other religious plans to remedy what didn't need healing, it left many young gays confused, in despair, and committing suicide.

A significant component of the books in this series will include an individual analysis of the killers. In some cases, the question of who the murderer was about will be examined – whether the murderer was about the person they desired or the person at the heart of the murder. From the killers' outlook, was their reason for committing murder different because of their sexual orientation? Or was the murder about the act of desiring them?

The answer to this question is entirely different when the victims are gay. After all, like any other minority group or class of people in the World, that fact creates a reason for some to want to kill them. The sexual component is complex, so that it will take several examples. Some cases involve both the killer and the victim being homosexual. In these particular cases, we can see quite a few similarities to that of heterosexual murderers. We will find emotional perspectives to be the major causes of the murders. The motive could be anything from jealousy to unreciprocated love or the actual murderer unable to find love due to mental issues or social circumstances. But most importantly, in all those cases, the type of love, albeit homosexual or heterosexual, is only the affections of such devotion.

In this fourth edition of the *Killer Queens* book series, we visit Canada. The previous books looked at murders in the gay communities of Germany, England, and the United States. To make the cases fully understood by readers, I have to describe the country, society, and how gay people are seen in those places. After all, the communities' reaction will primarily be based on their opinions of gays, not just in the legal sense but the moral beliefs as well.

In the early nineteen hundreds, Germany saw an actual move toward allowing gays to live more freely than in other countries. Even though it was still illegal, police had been giving out passes to those who were gay, including men who wanted to dress and live as a female. There was even a successful sex-change surgery in Germany in 1924.

Meanwhile, at the same time in the United States, during the tale of Leopold & Loeb, gay people were primarily perceived as sick and having an illness that needed to be cured. Not like any other illness, such as the flu, where you need plenty of rest, fluids, and care from others. The gay sickness people essentially looked at with anger. It was bad behavior, and the community essentially wanted to punish gays.

In current day England, London's significant metropolitan capital, being gay is now legal and no longer considered a sickness. Yet, the police detectives in that city allowed several gay men to be murdered and raped for years without attempting an essential investigation. It wasn't until the media got involved with supporting murder victims' families that Stephen Port, the "Grindr Serial Killer," was caught.

Canada has been one of the first countries to make it legal to be gay—even legalizing gay marriages and giving same-sex benefits. The country has seemed to embrace the gay community overall. So, you might wonder why I would include a gay serial killer who lived and worked in a country with no issues with his gay lifestyle? That's simple. As much as this series wants to point out the negative aspects of murders in the gay community in countries that don't respect gay people, it's essential to show its effects in countries that support gay people. Does it harm their reputation? Does anything within that country change because of the murders among the gay communities?

INTRODUCTION

In January 2019, Bruce McArthur, a 67-year-old Canadian landscaper, was convicted of eight first-degree murders and sentenced to life imprisonment. During the seven years between 2010 and 2017, McArthur preyed on men from Toronto's gay community and managed to avoid any detection by carefully cutting the bodies of his victims into pieces and burying them in the pot planters and grounds of his landscaping customers. His victims included Selim Esen, Andrew Kinsman, Majeed Kayhan, Dean Lisowick, Soroush Mahmudi, Skandaraj Navaratnam, Abdulbasir Faizi, and Kirushna Kanagaratnam. Additional charges were later placed on McArthur after an expanded investigation of hundreds of missing persons and deaths during those years.

During the first two years of gay men going missing, the LGBTQ community of Toronto suspected that there was someone stalking men in their community. The police didn't feel there was any evidence of this until, in 2012, 42-year-old Faizi, 40-year-old Navaratnam, and 58-year-old Kayhan went missing. By November that year, police launched an investigation called "Houston" into the gay men who were missing. After two years with no results, they closed the investigation.

Three years later, in 2017, after 49-year-old Kinsman and 44-year-old Esen went missing, police launched another Prism investigation. The police spent four months discovering the remains of each victim and forensically identifying them. When the study finally ended, there were over 1800 pieces of evidence from searches of over 100 properties.

McArthur's reign of terror on the gay village of Toronto finally ended on January 17, 2018, when police arrested and eventually charged him with the eight murders.

This type of crime leads to many questions. Does it still affect law enforcement when the victims of crimes and murder are gay? I don't mean this personally. More specifically, do the detectives take a different approach to their process when trying to solve murders of gay people? I am confident that there will always be a certain percentage of police officers, just as in general society, who do not agree with the lifestyle or simply do not like gay people. In those cases, we have to hope as a society that the overall police departments still do their job in solving crimes and not let those few detectives get in the way.

Similar to the previous three books in this series, we look into the gay community of, in this case, Toronto and the overall feeling within the country toward gay people. We need to check the laws and see what the government does with these cases.

McArthur was first convicted of assault in 2003 after assaulting a man with an iron pipe in 2001. He soon began working for a friend who had a landscaping company, and after a few years, he bought out his partner and went on his own with the company. He said he hired part-time helpers until one of them disappeared. To maintain this persona of an ordinary man, McArthur also played Santa Claus at Toronto's Agincourt Mall for two or three years.

McArthur approached his victims with great caution. He killed them with a rope and metal bar, which he used to tighten the ligature, causing strangulation. After the victim died, he posed them and took pictures, usually in his Thorncliffe Park Drive 19th floor apartment. Once, he used his red Dodge Caravan when he posed his victim in a fur coat and a cigar in his mouth.

Before taking pictures of his victims, he shaved their heads and facial hair, such as their beards. Then he took close-up images of their genitals. In some cases, when he took their photos, a few still had the metal pipe and rope tied around their necks. He had to shave them entirely after they died while leaving the ligature around their necks before he took the photos. McArthur kept his pictures of his dead victims in digital files on his computer to relive his kills anytime he felt the need. After taking the photos of his victims, he dismembered their bodies. Their body parts ended up distributed in the garden or lawns of his clients.

Even though the gay community in Canada by far has more laws and rights to protect them within the country, why were these missing person cases left for so long? Why were there no real investigations covering these men who went missing?

Hopefully, this book will shed some light on these questions, but I can't help but think that even though a law changes and a country can support a group of people like the gay community, it takes time for people to grow and change their beliefs. If you lived and worked in a country where it was illegal and a bad thing to be gay since you were born, it would take time to change and not only accept the legal changes but to learn to move forward with the changes.

PART I

BACKGROUND

TORONTO GAY VILLAGE

Toronto is the most populated city in all of Canada and the fourth largest city in North America, with a population of about three million and a greater area of almost seven million people. Twenty-nine miles of the town sits on the shore of Lake Ontario, one of the Great Lakes, with slightly sloping hills throughout. The Church-Wellesley Village, commonly called the Toronto Gay Village, offers the LGBTQ community a small-town feel with inclusiveness and safety for all within the busy city of Toronto. The neighborhood is the center of businesses that cater to the gay community. The community has expanded tremendously over the last twenty years. Many of the gay community also live in outlying neighborhoods such as The Annex,

Cabbagetown, St. James Town, St. Lawrence, Riverdale, and the Garden District.

Part of the area was once the estate of Alexander Wood, infamously known as "Molly Wood's Bush." Wood was an importer of goods from London and Scotland after immigrating to Toronto from Scotland in 1793. He was eventually appointed as a magistrate for the city in 1801. He served in this position until 1810 when he was disgraced by a sex scandal in which he was involved.

The scandal started when Wood began an investigation on a reported rape case. The victim approached Wood, claiming that she was raped and didn't know the identity of her attacker. The only evidence she could offer Wood was that when the assailant was raping her, she had a chance to grab and scratch his penis. As part of the investigation, Wood decided to inspect the penises of every possible suspect the police named as the potential assailant.

During Wood's inspection of the penises, he asked the men to strip down completely naked and stand before him. After entering the room, he asked the men to lay down, grab their genitals, and rub them until they became aroused. Wood claimed that this was the only way he could make a thorough search of their penises to determine if there were any scratches on them. However, the people around town didn't see it that way, and there was a lot of talk about how inappropriate Wood had been to the suspected men. Rumors started, grew, and eventually changed to the point where the people declared that there never was a rape case. It was widely believed that Wood only made the case up so that he could feel other men's genitals and perhaps even seduce them into sex.

Judge William Drummer Powell, who was also Wood's good friend, had the task of approaching him about the rumors around town. If there was any truth to them, there was a good chance that Wood would be charged with sodomy. Wood quickly denied the charges to Powell. But it wasn't long before Wood got the nickname "Molly Wood"—"molly" was a derogatory slang term for homosexuals. Within wealthier and more refined people, he was called the "Inspector of Private Accounts." Powell claimed he didn't believe the charges against Wood and suggested that it might be better if Wood left town for a few years – just until people forgot about the stories and moved on to gossip about other things. Powell aided in making the complaints that came forward to the court disappear. Wood became so overwhelmed and upset with the rumors and people laughing at him behind his back that he took up Powell's offer and went back to Scotland for a while to let things calm down.

Just two years later, in 1812, Wood returned to Toronto, and he was given his magistrate position again. The War of 1812 had just begun and took the nation's full attention away from his scandal. In 1823, Wood was recommended to be appointed a place on the 1812 War Commission, but Judge Powell refused to appoint him because of his 1810 scandal. It was then that Wood finally realized that Powell had it in for him all along and probably even helped spread the rumors about him back then.

Wood sued Powell for defamation of his character and won. Wood bought 50 acres of land around his home on Yonge Street, and it became known as "Molly Wood's Bush." Wood lived the rest of his life there until 1842 when he became ill. He then returned home to Scotland, where he died at age 72. He was never married, nor did he have any children.

The area known as Molly Wood's Bush is now part of the Church and Wellesley gay village today. A statue of him was erected in 2005. Prior to 1969, before it was legal, there was an underground gay male scene that included taverns, bathhouses, and steam rooms that were not advertised as being gay. They had straight clientele but were known as places to go if you were gay and wanted to meet other gay men. The Allan Gardens became the park where gay men would go to meet other gay men. The Church Street area has remained the primary gay area of Toronto from then on.

In the seventies and eighties, gay establishments were allowed to open to the public, so several gay bars, coffee shops, and businesses began to open in this area. After that, the gay community started having drag shows which drew those against allowing gay people their freedoms. They threw things like eggs and tomatoes at the performers. During this period, there was no police support for the gay community. Before the law changed, the police constantly arrested gay people for being gay. Just because the law changed, their feelings wouldn't change that quickly. The community kept on moving forward, and businesses kept on opening up.

OPERATION SOAP

The Toronto Police Department planned to raid the four gay bathhouses in 1981. They dubbed it "Operation Soap," and it was the largest police operation in years. Two hundred police officers arrested over 300 men. During the 1970s, police had undertaken several small raids on bathhouses or steambaths, but it was nothing compared to this operation. Typically, only two to four officers would walk through one bath house and try to intimidate the men who were there to leave the premises with the threat of arrest. If anybody ever challenged an officer, he would be struck and arrested.

These smaller raids were primarily meant to scare the men at the bathhouse. They knew most men there were married and living straight lives, so they didn't want to get arrested. So they just took the abuse. Also, if they embarrassed enough of the men there, they might not return. They were hoping the business would eventually go broke. These small raids were just a way to let the officers who were into bullying people or simply power-hungry assert their authority over others who could not fight back.

The Operation Soap raids began on February 5, 1981 at 11 p.m. eastern time. Police simultaneously raided four downtown Toronto bathhouses, including Club Baths, The Romans Spa, The Richmond Health Emporium, and The Barracks. Police entered the steam baths armed with hammers and crowbars, which they used to break open all the lockers in the change rooms. They herded the men outside in the winter cold, whether they wore clothing, had a towel, or were naked. The men were rounded up and questioned about their wives, where they worked, and the names of their bosses. The police were intimidating the men, already in a vulnerable position, by screaming obscenities at them.

The Roman Spa was a 21 and older-only club, mainly where men could meet each other and use private rooms to engage in sex, but no money was exchanged. Club Toronto was much the same, but police kicked down and destroyed 20 of the 57 doors that belonged to their private rooms during the raid. The Richmond Street Health Emporium would be so bad that the owners couldn't afford to reopen after that. The last club raided, The Barracks, reopened a few months later only because it had several owners who could afford to fix the damage done by the police during the raid.

In total, twenty of these establishments' owners were arrested and charged with keeping a typical bawdy house, and 306 men were charged for being caught there. The old bawdy house laws were aimed at places where prostitution occurred. Prostitution meant some money was exchanged for sex, but there was no money in these bathhouses. These venues were just a place where men met to date. The police decision to raid these venues was solely a blatant way to abuse gay men.

After the raids, many in the gay community blamed the attack on a CBC documentary shown the previous month, which told the stories of gay men and why they went to these clubs. On January 15th, the CBC aired a 90-minute television special, *Sharing the Secret: Select Gay Stories.* The documentary followed several gay men and covered their personal stories. According to the program, these men had a sexual proclivity that was supposed to be shared by about ten percent of the population. But for these men to practice their deviancy, they had to go to bathhouses or steam rooms.

It turned out that the documentary wasn't about learning what it was like to be a gay man and sharing this with the public. Instead, it was more about trying to shock its 1981 audience into fearing that someone in your family could perhaps catch this disease and there was no cure. It upset much of the public. It alleged that you could be stuck with your family member forever cruising parks, bathrooms, and bathhouses for transient sex with other men. And that your children could be in danger. You certainly had to keep these men away from your children.

Most men arrested in Operation Soap were charged with being caught in a bawdy house or owning one. A "Bawdy House" was a legal term that covered houses of prostitution that didn't fit the bathhouses, even though there was never any money exchanged for sex. The police knew these places were not prostitution businesses, so they tried using a different interpretation of the law from a part written in the statute that describes the sex in these places as 'indecent.' The businesses were still fined heavily, up to $40,000. These laws remained in effect until 2015 but were rarely used after this raid.

Like everything we live through, one outrage leads to an action and then a counter-fury. Accordingly, the documentary aired on television, which sparked anger in the general public. The police responded by conducting a large raid to round up these 'perverts' and clean up the city. After people saw and heard the stories about what happened during these raids, instead of being happy, they became angry about how it was done. There were several rallies and protests against the actions of the police. The protests were what became known as the Toronto Pride Parade— Canada's equivalent to the 1969 Stonewall Riots in America.

People in the city were in shock since the raids on the news made Canada look like it was a police state and something you would see in a communist country. The upset led to over 3000 people rallying to protest the arrests. They blocked the traffic at many significant intersections and had mass rallies. A Legal Defense Committee was formed after the raids to raise money for the arrested men so they could afford a lawyer to represent them in court. There were another 30 lawyers who defended men for no charge.

Two years later, in April of 1983, almost 90 percent of the men charged for being in a bathhouse had been acquitted, and the 36 initially found guilty were given discharges. The few other remaining charges were settled with plea bargains. Most of these charges were dropped because the officers who made the arrests could not identify any of the men they arrested. Some men also claimed they were there to work out at the gym and use the pool in the bathhouse. Not everyone there came for sex, and the police couldn't identify any men who were there having sex when they entered the clubs.

On Wednesday, June 15, 2016, Toronto Police Chief Mark Saunders made a surprising apology for the police raids of 1981. It was unheard of. He also apologized for another raid on Club Toronto in 2000, where police claimed it was to search for any alcohol on the premises. Later in 2005, the police were sued for this raid and settled out of court.

These raids were conducted simply because gay men were a group that had no human rights, and the police could treat them any way that they wanted to. The raids not only gave these men a criminal record just for being gay, but they also got them fired from their jobs, caused problems with their friends and families, and even led to divorce in some cases because of the public exposure.

An unexpected and good thing came from the 1981 raids—it brought the gay community together and led to considerable support from the public. The average person living in Toronto, and even Canada, didn't know what a bathhouse was, so it was a learning experience for the whole country.

Even though homosexuality was legal in 1969, many men still couldn't come out to the public for myriad reasons. Many could lose their jobs or families, so joining a private club to meet other men for sex was appealing. It also saved them from having to go out to a public establishment and perhaps be seen by someone they knew.

One of the theories that remain today was that the raids were politically motivated. Many political leaders and the police hated an openly gay activist of the time, George Hislop. He was the first gay person to run for the city council and had gained a considerable following. He also happened to be one of the owners of the Barracks—one of the clubs raided in Operation Soap. Conservatives in the country also wanted the area cleaned up, which meant it was time to clean up the gay part of town. To them, all things gay were terrible. Either they believed that being gay was dirty and an illness, or it was against God's law. They undoubtedly, at the very minimum, wanted to slow down its growth in the public and stop people from trying to make it "okay" in society. They believed it could influence the children to behave 'gay.' So, in their minds, raiding these bathhouses would not only clean up the city but also get people to rally behind the cause of stopping homosexuality.

Gay bathhouse and health club raids had been going on before and even continued after Operation Soap. The constant fear of being caught in one of these raids was very real for men. And became more so each time it happened and made the news. Here are just some of the more well-known police raids on record:

- In December 1978, the Barracks were raided, and 23 men were arrested and charged for indecent sexual acts in a bawdy house. During this raid, the men claimed police called them derogatory names such as "faggot," "queer," and "weirdos."
- In October 1979, police not only raided a bathhouse but also raided five apartments in the nearby Toronto downtown area, plus a cottage in Percy, Ontario. This raid resulted in 27 men charged with indecent sex acts under the bawdy-house laws.

- Just four months after the Operation Soap raids in June 1981, police raided the Back Door and charged eight of the men found there.

These types of raids continued until September 2000, when police ran an undercover operation on Club Toronto. This raid ended with a lawsuit that the police not only settled but also a promise to start a new training program for officers of all ranks to learn how to deal with gay, lesbian, and transgender people during their interactions.

BRUCE MCARTHUR

Bruce McArthur | Facebook Image

Bruce McArthur was born on October 8, 1951, in Lindsay, Ontario, and grew up on a farm in the Kawartha Lakes region of rural Ontario with his parents and older sister. His father came from Scotland, and his mother was of Irish descent. His parents ran a farm and would take troubled kids from the urban Toronto area and offered them a nice place to live in return for working the farm.

Bruce was often left to manage all the kids that had come to the farm to live and work. He resented having to work with all the other kids and train them how to work a farm. He felt his father knew he was gay and thought putting him to work with manual labor would change him into a man.

Religion was an issue in the McArthur household. They were unsure of what religion they should teach all the children. Bruce's mother was Catholic, while his father was Presbyterian. The different religions led to several heated arguments about whose faith was the right religion. Bruce would always take his mother's side in these fights, which caused even more of a separation between him and his dad.

Bruce graduated high school in June of 1969, even though he found it a struggle to get through. He wasn't an outstandingly behaved student since he only got average grades. But other students had known him as the teacher's pet. After high school, he took a two-year business course at a Barrie college, where he met his future wife, Janice. After graduating in 1973, they moved into a high-rise apartment in Toronto.

McArthur's first job in Toronto was working for Eaton's Department store selling men's socks and underwear. By 1978 he became a sales representative for one of the manufacturers, McGregor Sock Company, where his work region covered the province of Ontario. With his new job, he would be responsible for servicing all the stores that sold that brand of socks and underwear.

During this time, Bruce's father was placed in an assisted living facility due to a brain tumor that left him unable to care for himself. Bruce traveled to visit his father at the facility, and he later claimed the two ended up being the closest they had ever been.

His mother ended up living with another man in the family home where McArthur grew up, leaving Bruce so angry that he would no longer speak to her. The two of them never reconciled. She died only one year later of cancer.

Bruce married Janice in 1979, and they moved to the suburb of Oshawa, Ontario, which was about 60 kilometers away from Toronto, and they had two children. McArthur changed from Catholic to Presbyterian and attended a local church with his family.

McArthur had sexual desires for men but wanted to keep them a secret. He started to meet men on the newly created internet chatrooms as he was too scared to go to a park or restroom and get caught cruising other men or having sex.

In the early 1990s, McArthur started having casual affairs with other men he met. At the same time, he decided to stop having sex with his wife, not only because he didn't want to have sex with her, but because he did not want to give her any sexual diseases.

After McArthur started to get comfortable and more accepting of his sexuality being gay, he decided he would tell his wife and kids about it. The family was shocked to hear about his feelings but didn't disown or stop talking to him. McArthur and his wife stayed together until 1997, when McArthur decided to move out and get an apartment in Toronto. McArthur wanted to have his place to bring men home and have some privacy. He couldn't do this in the same house where his ex-wife and kids lived. Not only would he feel uncomfortable having sex with men in his room and be worried about them making too much noise and everyone hearing them. But most of the men he had met were people he didn't know, so he wouldn't be able to trust bringing them to the house where his family lived.

During these years, McArthur was dealing with the financial stress from his marriage and their son Todd, who found himself in trouble at school and at home.

Shortly after McArthur moved into his apartment, he met another man who had a similar life and came out later in his life too. The two of them decided to live together, and he moved in with McArthur at his apartment in the Thorncliffe Park area of town.

Money issues and a bad investment led to McArthur filing for bankruptcy at the beginning of 1999. He was also facing the 'coming out' process among the people he worked with and at his church. He ended up leaving the church after they couldn't accept his new lifestyle of living with another man.

His relationship with the man ended after only two years. McArthur wanted the couple to become committed to each other and monogamous, and a total commitment, but his partner didn't want that. He was struggling with McArthur's financial issues, bankruptcy, and his son's issues with the law. McArthur's son Todd often ended up staying with the couple as he continued to get into legal problems. The police would only release him if he had a stable home to which to go. McArthur's live-in didn't like this.

They broke up but continued to live in the same apartment. McArthur eventually ended up seeing a psychiatrist and started taking the antidepressant Prozac to function correctly in his life.

That same year in 1999, McArthur started

dating a new love interest of his, a man named Skanda.

3

FIRST BLOOD 2001

On the afternoon of October 31, 2001, Mark Henderson was on his way home from shopping for his party outfit for the evening festivities that always took place around the gay village on Halloween. When he reached the outside front door of his apartment building, he gradually managed to open the door while juggling the day's shopping bags.

As Henderson managed to get to the door, he turned and saw Bruce McArthur running up the sidewalk towards the front door. Thinking that McArthur must know somebody in the building, or perhaps he was there to look at an apartment that was up for rent, he held the door open with his body, and McArthur entered the building.

Henderson followed McArthur into the lobby

and headed down the hall towards his apartment, not paying attention to which way McArthur was going. He continued to his apartment's front door, put his bags on the floor, and began to unlock his door when suddenly, Henderson felt a crash come across his back. He immediately turned around to find McArthur standing behind him, holding a metal pipe over his head. Before he could say anything, McArthur hit him with the pipe again, this time right over his head.

Henderson previously worked as a nurse, and when he saw blood and spinal fluid pouring down his face, he knew he could go unconscious any minute. So, he started to yell loudly, dragging himself into his apartment as fast as he could, knowing that if he did pass out, he'd be done. Henderson grabbed the phone to call 911 while McArthur ran out of the apartment building, startled by Henderson's yelling. Police arrived and took the basic description of his assailant. Henderson was taken to the hospital, where he had a compound fracture on his skull and a broken finger which took six months to recover.

Meanwhile, at a nearby police precinct, McArthur entered and went to the front desk to report that he had just committed an assault on someone. He was arrested and charged with assault with a dangerous weapon causing bodily harm. The two men were not friends and had no real history together. They knew who each other was but never talked. Henderson would later say that he didn't like McArthur, so he never spoke to him.

The assault did not go to trial until 2003. The prosecution described the assault as McArthur getting into a scuffle with a known prostitute. They made it sound like they fought over payment for services or something like that. It was ridiculous but enough to taint the court and paint an image of the victim.

Even though Henderson had worked all sorts of jobs, including being a nurse and a model who had been clean and sober for over ten years before the assault, it was too late. The prosecutor continued to call Henderson a 'known sex worker' during the whole trial just because he had an arrest on his record in the nineteen-eighties for solicitation. Henderson hadn't done anything like that since then, and the encounter had nothing to do with them meeting for any reason. He just let McArthur into the apartment building in which he lived.

The prosecutor suggested that when Henderson opened the outside door to the apartment building after seeing McArthur out in front of the street, and when Henderson held the door open for McArthur, it was an offer for him to come into his apartment and for the two of them to have sex. After all, it was still quite common for any law enforcement officer to think that homosexuals would jump at any chance with any man to have sex any chance that they had.

McArthur also claimed that he carried the metal pipe to protect himself against the aggressive pan-handlers or prostitutes known to rob people often. McArthur eventually pleaded guilty to 8 assault charges but couldn't give any reason for the attack. He apologized to Henderson for causing him so much pain and anguish. The Court ordered a psychological evaluation of McArthur before the judge sentenced him.

The psychological report was returned to the Court a few weeks later, and it said that McArthur was not likely to re-offend. The stress that he had been under from his divorce, financial issues, and his son's legal problems probably caused him to snap. Also, in the report, McArthur claimed to have lost consciousness, and when he came to, Mark was already lying on the floor, unconscious and bleeding. He claimed to have only been on it about six months before the attack.

The psychological report concluded that there were no signs of any psychosis and no traces of any drug that could have made him delusional. The report also said that McArthur was very well-orientated and knew where he lived and what time he lived in, showing that he wasn't suffering from antisocial behaviors. Nothing in the report suggested that McArthur had any personality disorders, and he had no reasons for his behavior. Therefore, it was concluded that McArthur's high anxiety caused him to snap and attack someone. They also thought that it was highly improbable that he would assault anyone like this again.

Instead of the possible ten-year sentence, McArthur only received one year of house arrest, in which he could leave his home to go to work or a pre-approved appointment, such as a doctor. He also had a two-year ban from going into the gay village in Toronto, followed by three years' probation. Under no circumstances was McArthur to use amyl nitrite, commonly known as a popper, to heighten sexual pleasure by relaxing the muscles in the body. He would also have to attend an anger management course and perform one hundred hours of community service.

The lenient sentence imposed on McArthur put fear and sadness into the victim, Henderson. He had to live with knowing that McArthur not only hadn't been punished for his crime, but he was allowed to walk freely in the city. And who was to say that McArthur wouldn't attack him again. He suffered long-term emotional damage from the attack. Despite the fear, Henderson faced things headfirst by becoming an auxiliary police officer in 2007. He built a new trust between police and the gay community in that role. But during an altercation at the 2016 Pride event, he was attacked. The police who investigated didn't care enough to make a police report or investigate the case, so he resigned.

MCARTHUR FULFILLED all of his probation requirements. After completing everything, he applied for a pardon which would clear his criminal record from the public. Later, in 2014, he received it.

In 2002, after McArthur was released from his house arrest, he started taking different jobs with clothing companies, but they wouldn't last. He was either laid off or quit over the frustration of starting from scratch with each company again. He was finding it hard to work himself up again. During this time, he had to rely on his ex-boyfriend, who he was still living with, to pay for everything.

Roger Horan, a landscaping company owner, was looking for a person to buy into the business and become his partner. He was by trade a designer and not a gardener, so he was looking for someone who could do the actual landscaping work. He soon met McArthur at a gay event, and the two started Artistic Design Limited.

Horan marketed the company and found clients, while McArthur did the landscaping. They eventually gained a reputation for creating beautiful landscapes and became quite popular in the area. They became so busy that McArthur had to start buying lots of equipment like lawn mowers and trimmers but had no place to keep them as he was still living in an apartment. One of his family's friends, Karen Fraser, hired him to do her landscaping, and when she found out that he needed some space to keep his lawn equipment, she offered him an empty double garage that she had as a place for him to store his equipment, in exchange for free landscaping.

McArthur also worked as Santa Claus in the local shopping mall over Christmas and the off-season, in addition to his landscaping work.

In 2006, after McArthur completed his probation and community service, he went out again to the clubs and bars in the gay community. Around that time, his son was getting into trouble with the law and often ended up at McArthur's apartment. McArthur then started to make his son work for the landscaping business to try and keep him out of trouble.

Along with his son Todd, McArthur hired other young men to work for him, usually ones of

Asian or Arab ethnicity. One such employee ended up being Skanda. Rumors were that McArthur was having a sexual relationship with Skanda and the two even spent some evenings together. Skanda was not the type to settle down with one person, so tensions ensued as McArthur was looking for a partner, so the relationship wasn't going the way McArthur had hoped it would.

PART II

THE MURDERS

4

SKANDARAJ "SKANDA" NAVARATNAM 2010

Skandaraj, known as "Skanda," was last seen leaving the Zipperz nightclub in Toronto on September 10, 2010, around 2 a.m. At the time, the forty-year-old was out on his regular Friday night route, visiting with regular guests and employees of the club. It was the start of the Labor Day long weekend, so Skanda started the evening by going to the Black Eagle's barbeque before hitting Zipperz. He was seen leaving with an unknown man. It was thought they were probably going for something to eat or perhaps to one of their homes. But this was unusual for Skanda as he was a trendy and social guy in the community.

Skanda was thrilled to be in Canada, where he was allowed to be himself as an out gay man. He had to move away from Sri Lanka just a few years earlier. In 2008, Skanda came out to his brothers. He was the second oldest of four. Eventually, the three of them left for Canada together, not only for the possibility of living a better life but to protect their brother from being religiously persecuted.

Skanda started working as a research assistant at the University of Toronto just a few months earlier, near the end of June. He got a puppy, a husky, which he walked throughout the gay village. These walks became a large part of his social activity since it was there that he met several other gay people who also had their dogs out for walks.

The brothers kept the fact that Skanda was missing from their mother back in Sri Lanka. She was never told about his being gay, as she was now eighty years old and had a bad heart. The brothers didn't want her to worry. They were afraid they would kill her from the shock of finding out that Skanda was not only gay but that he was now missing.

It was almost a week before Skanda's friends decided to report him missing to the police. He had up and disappeared without warning before. He was known to take off to one of his friend's cottages or go camping. On one of his previous 'vanishing' trips, he ended up at a Buddhist Monastery in Niagara Falls. This time was different. His friends knew him well enough to know that he wouldn't just leave his new puppy alone without somebody to ensure he was fed and had water.

In January 2018, when the report of Bruce McArthur's arrest was publicized, one of Skanda's brothers contacted the detective in charge of Skanda's disappearance case. It was another seven long years of waiting for any answers about their brother before they received any news. And the news was alarming—it looked like McArthur and Skanda were linked romantically.

One of Skanda's friends in the Toronto gay village, Kevin Nash, said he felt something wasn't right between them. One year before Skanda went missing, he ran into him in a bathhouse, and the two talked about what had been happening in their lives. Skanda had just begun dating McArthur at the time, and Nash was surprised to see him in a bathhouse. Usually, when you are first with someone, you spend all of your free time with them. In Nash's mind, Skanda must not have been thrilled with McArthur; perhaps he was hiding out there.

Nash claimed that when he saw Skanda, he grabbed him and took him into a private room to find out what was happening. Skanda looked scared and wouldn't look Nash directly in the eye. Nash wanted to know if his new date, McArthur, had hurt him, but Skanda told him that nothing had happened to him but was scared of how he would burst into weird, violent rages.

Nash gave Skanda his phone number and told him to call if he needed help. Nash knew there was no way that Skanda would go to the police for any reason as he was a gay immigrant from Sri Lanka. He had a distrust for any authority figure after his experiences there, and he wanted to stay out of any trouble. The next and last time Nash would see Skanda was when he saw him leaving a gay bar on Church Street with McArthur.

Nash met Skanda in 1994 when Skanda was dating one of his friends. Skanda was known as a person who loved to laugh and had great charisma.

5

ABDULBASIR "BASIR" FAIZI 2010

On December 30, 2010, Kareema Faizi walked into the Peel Regional Police Department to report that her husband, Abdulbasir, usually known as "Basir," hadn't returned home from his job the previous night. Kareema last talked to Basir on the phone that evening when he called her from work. He seemed normal and in good spirits. Basir, Kareema, and their two daughters were all looking forward to going on a vacation the next month. Kareema claimed they were pleased as a family, and Basir was not depressed or upset. He spent all of his time with his family or working.

Kareema couldn't think of any enemies he had or any reason for somebody to kidnap him. They didn't have any money or wealth as Basir had to claim bankruptcy just a few years before. He would also never be involved in anything illegal, Kareema told police.

Basir was born in Herat, Afghanistan, in the early 1970s. When the Soviet Union invaded the country in 1979, Basir had to become part of the military and join the fighting against the Russians. There was a civil war in the country, and the Taliban began to take control. In 1999, Basir married Kareema, and they started to raise a family. They had two daughters. As the country's situation worsened, and after twenty years of war, they decided to flee to Canada in early 2000.

The family found a home in Brampton, Ontario, and Basir got a job for a local label printing company, close to where they settled. Basir was making a decent living but wanted to set something up so that he could retire from work before he got too old. So, along with a friend, he bought two properties that were used as an investment they could rent. Within a year, the friend he had invested in the properties with took the money they had earned from the rentals and left town. Just after that, Basir was laid off from his job. Basir ended up claiming bankruptcy after this.

Basir went into a deep depression after everything happened, and he wanted to move to another city to get a fresh start. He wanted to go to a place where nobody knew who he was or what had happened. He was looking at Ottawa as it was a city large enough in which to get lost. Another probability was that he would find it easier to deal with his other side—the gay side. He would have places to go to where he could meet men.

Basir became a regular at the Toronto nightclubs Zipperz and the Black Eagle, which were popular among the Gay leather community. When Basir didn't have much time, he often skipped the regular nightclubs and headed right for Steamworks, a bathhouse where he could go and have quick sex with other men and get home without being too late.

After having sex with anonymous men, he often made it a point to go to Salaam Canada, a public group for gay Muslims, where they would have meetings, discuss their issues, and get counseling.

The police went to their home and took the family's computer to see if any information could explain Basir's disappearance. They discovered he had left his passport at home and had no credit cards. A few days later, the police found his car parked and abandoned.

Kareema sent emails or called all their friends they knew, but nobody had heard from him.

A few weeks later, detectives called her into the detachment to explain the details of what they had learned about her husband and what they figured had happened to him. It seems that on the night he was supposed to be working and called her, he was out at the Black Eagle in Toronto. He had met a friend there, and the two of them went to Steamworks. It was about 11:30 p.m. Shortly after, he went to a burger eatery and bought some food, as they had the transaction from his bank card. Basir told his friend that he was heading home when they were finished for the evening.

Detectives concluded that Basir had left his wife and family for another person. And the person was probably a man. From their computer search, they discovered that he had been living a double life and had several extramarital affairs with several men.

Kareema was in shock, and again, she contacted all of their friends and family members to find out if any of them knew anything about Basir's homosexuality. None of them had. Even with all of this new information, she held hope that she would find him. She went to the gay village, constantly searching for him and showing his picture to anyone who would stop and look.

A few months later, Kareema filed for divorce, claiming that she thought Basir had abandoned her and his daughters emotionally and financially.

6

MAJEED "HAMID" KAYHAN 2012

In July 2016, almost six years after Majeed "Hamid" Kayhan went missing, the police found his remains. Fifty-eight-year-old Kayhan was the last of the eight victims of Bruce McArthur to be seen.

His remains were the only ones found in a forested ravine behind a Mallory Crescent home where McArthur had worked as a landscaper. The other seven victims' remains were discovered in large planters at a Leaside home, where McArthur worked landscaping and gardening for the owners. Why Kayhan was singled out and placed in a different location is still unknown to police.

Majeed was also born in Afghanistan, not far from the Iranian border. He was raised a strict Muslim as his father was a priest. In 1983, he married and had two children. After the war broke out, he, too, moved to Canada with his family in early 2000.

His new home kept him and his family safe. But it also opened the door to his "inner demons," as he thought of it, and he started going to the gay district of downtown Toronto. There, he would identify himself as Hamid, his real middle name, but not the name by which his family or work knew him.

Hamid started spending much of his free time at a Turkish steam bath called the Oak Leaf in Toronto. This steam bath was known as a place to go to if you wanted to experiment with men sexually, and Hamid thought it was a perfect place to act on his feelings. It took about two years for him to find a partner and decide that he would move in with the man in his City Park apartment and file for divorce from his wife.

Even though Hamid was out in the downtown part of Toronto, he wanted to keep it secret from his family and work friends. He was scared of how he would be treated and didn't want to lose contact with his children or job. After living in Afghanistan for so long, he had the instinct to keep things like this secret.

Even though Hamid was now free to be himself, he carried tremendous guilt that quickly threw him into severe depression. He would often drink himself unconscious. He often went to the Black Eagle, to their dark upstairs room, and had many sexual encounters until he passed out. This behavior contrasted sharply with when he entered the club singing show tunes.

Hamid also had a problem with simply talking with people on a friendly basis. He was lonely and wanted to make a deeper connection with another man. It seemed he had to drink a lot of alcohol to approach people, and it would only be in a place like a bathhouse.

Hamid often tried to quit drinking alcohol cold turkey, which caused him to be very angry, and he would get into major fights with his live-in boyfriend. The emotional turmoil eventually led Hamid to try methamphetamines which were widely used and available in the gay bathhouses. The drugs were primarily used to help relax men and heighten their sexual experience, but for Hamid, it became a way of life, and he became addicted.

In mid-October 2016, Hamid took the subway

out to the North part of the city to attend a family wedding. He had a large extended family and had to keep up the appearance of being a stable working man to keep a relationship open with his children. After the ceremony, Hamid was dropped off at the subway station, and his family never heard from him again. After a week of trying to get hold of Hamid and being unsuccessful, Hamid's son went to his father's apartment to find his father's pet birds all dead at the bottom of their cage. He reported his father missing to the police on October 28th.

7

ZAMBIAN MEAT WEBSITE

The first known case covering the exploits surrounding the *Zambian Meat* website came to light in Germany in November of 2013 when the police in Dresden arrested a 55-year-old for murdering, dismembering, and eating another man after meeting on this website. *Zambian Meat*, now defunct, was a chat forum-style website where men would go to discuss their fantasies of combining sex and cannibalism.

The police released a statement saying that the two men had met several times on the website for over three months until they met in person on November 4, 2012, at Dresden's Central Train Station. The two went to a guest house the killer owned in the Ore Mountains, near the Czechoslovakian border. The police thought the victim had been tied up, beaten, tortured, and killed. Later, he was cut up into several pieces and buried around his Bed & Breakfast property.

Later, it was discovered by the media that the 55-year-old man arrested was a police officer identified only as "Detlev G." We found out later that the "G" stood for Guenzel. The officer was arrested while on the job, where he gave a partial confession but wouldn't say why he did it. He initially told police that the two men met on the *Zambian Meat* website, where the man had asked Guenzel to kill and eat him afterward. After a few months of interaction through emails, texts, and phone calls, the two met at the train station so that he could fulfill the man's fantasy.

In December 2016, he was found guilty of murder and disturbing a dead body and sentenced to eight years in prison. During the trial, Detlev G. admitted they met to have sex. The two men had got into an argument where Detlev stabbed the victim. Later, when he found the man dead, he decided to chop the body up into parts and dispose of it on the grounds. His defense lawyer said that the victim hanged himself, and Detlev had nothing to do with his death.

Zambian Meat was a site where members discussed fantasies primarily about eating or being eaten by another person. Most people on a website forum like this are known as "howlers."

They fantasize about cannibalism but are never into really doing it. They were considered no harm to anyone.

On the website, you saw a completely black screen with several gross images of human body parts and a log of older conversations made by members, including detailed descriptions of eating human flesh. Names or titles used on the website were the "Long Pig," considered a possible victim, and a "Chef," who was a qualified cannibal. Then, there was the "Master Chef," who was not only a qualified cannibal but was able to butcher and prepare the human meat for consumption. It is uncertain exactly what it took to be considered qualified for this title.

During this time in the Winter of 2012, the Swiss police called the Toronto Police Department wanting to speak with the detective in charge of the case involving missing gay men from Toronto. There wasn't an open case, never mind a detective in charge, so they talked to Officer Debby Harris. This conversation was the first time she had heard of the *Zambian Meat* website and a group of people interested in exotic meat and cannibalism. What did this have to do with a missing Canadian gay man? Swiss police explained what they had learned during their investigation of the *Zambian Meat* site.

Their undercover officer signed up to the

website and pretended to be someone who wanted to be eaten by another person. It wasn't long before a person using the name "Kanibm" started chatting to the informant online. Kanibm told him that he would beat him if he could come to Slovakia. The Swiss police passed this information on to the Slovakian police, who then set up an investigation. Slovakian police set up a date and place to meet this Kanibm. Their undercover officer showed up at his apartment, where Kanibm tried to kill him. The police surveilling entered the building, and a gunfight ended with Kanibm dead. While searching his apartment, the police found several body parts in the man's fridge. Later, it was discovered that Kanibm's real name was Matej Curko, and he was responsible for at least two murders leading to cannibalism.

Another person on the *Zambian Meat* website who contacted the Swiss undercover officer went by the screen name of "Chefmate." Chefmate told anybody he talked to on the website that his name was John Jacobs, who lived in the Toronto, Canada, area. He also had plenty of firearms on hand as he was a hunter of animals but also loved to hunt humans. He claimed to have killed and eaten human flesh and loved its taste.

Chefmate had joined the *Zambian Meat* website in December 2008 and was looking to kill and eat only men. He had no interest in females. The

Swiss police searched the internet and Toronto newspapers to see if there had been any strange murders or victims of possible cannibalism in the area. They didn't find anything like that, but they did notice that there had been a series of missing gay men from the Toronto Gay Village, so they decided to contact the Toronto police detectives to let them know what information they had.

This information was heightened even more because of what had already been happening in Canada since May 2012. A viral video on the internet called *1 Lunatic, 1 Icepick* showed what looked like a man killing another man, cutting off different body parts, having sex with these body parts, and even eating them. The rumors were that it was filmed in Montreal, but nobody knew for sure. At first, most people who saw the video believed that it was fake, not an actual murder.

After the video came to light, packages with body parts wrapped in tissue started arriving in the mail of both the Liberal and Conservative Government parties of Canada. Shortly after, a human torso in a suitcase was found outside a Montreal apartment building. This suitcase would lead the police to search an apartment building. During that search, they found one apartment covered with blood. The apartment belonged to a man named Luka Magnotta.

Could Luka Magnotta also be responsible for

the missing gay men in Toronto? It seems police thought that because Magnotta had eaten some of his victims on film, he might be a member of the *Zambian Meat* website and might even know or work with someone in finding, killing, and eating a male victim from the area.

Once the video caught the eye of the R.C.M.P., they concluded that it was of an actual victim being killed and eaten. An arrest warrant for Magnotta was issued. Magnotta left the country and traveled to Europe, where he was eventually caught while sitting in a café watching the news about himself in Germany. He was deported back to Canada.

The first thing Detective Harris did was to find out who the screen name "Chefmate50" was. After the detectives found the attached email to that screen name was "chefmate50@yahoo.com," they obtained a court order to see who owned that email address. Chefmate ended up belonging to Alex Brunton, who was a 64-year-old man who lived in Peterborough, Ontario, with his wife and worked as a minor hockey league coach. Brunton also worked part-time at the suicide prevention hotline, counseling people who called in for help.

In Brunton's chats with other members, he mentioned "Nathan" several times, which was supposed to be another cannibal like himself. Brunton had also set up a meeting with this

Nathan where he met him at a strip club named Remington's. The police knew that Magnotta not only worked at Remington's as a stripper but also used the alias of Nathan. On top of that, Magnotta only lived a few minutes away from Brunton in Peterborough. Were the two men connected? Did they work together?

There was no evidence that cannibalism was connected to the missing men. Still, when officer Debby Harris brought her concerns about the missing gay men possibly being victims of cannibalism, the Toronto Police Department decided they would set up a task force to investigate her concerns. It was called "Project Houston."

8

PROJECT HOUSTON 2012

The first thing Detective Charles Coffey did was to create an account on the *Zambian Meat* website so that he could chat and possibly meet the man called Chefmate. He told everyone he met in the forum that he wanted to be slaughtered and eaten and needed to find a man who would do this to him.

It took Coffey a couple of tries before he was approved to be a website member. The website had a questionnaire to be completed by anyone who wanted to join. It asked several questions about cannibalism, and Coffey didn't know the correct terms or terminology commonly used among cannibals, so he had to research and learn how to talk and act online before he was finally approved to join.

About a month later, Brunton, known as Chefmate, made contact with Coffey. Once they began chatting, he learned that according to Chefmate, he had already killed, tasted, and eaten human meat. Under his description, he was also good at cooking and storing human flesh.

While these chats were happening, other detectives monitored Brunton everywhere, including his home and work. Police also put a tracking device on his vehicle so they would know any place he went that was out of the ordinary. They reported him to Homeland Security and had his passport flagged in case he decided to travel anywhere to possibly meet one of his contacts from the *Zambian Meat* website.

After detectives obtained a search warrant to remove Brunton's computers and electrical devices, they decided it would probably be better to sneak into his residence and make a copy of his hard drive. That way, Brunton wouldn't know that police were monitoring him.

In 2012, when school got out for the Christmas holiday, Brunton took his family to visit his in-laws, who lived about one hour away. The surveillance team entered his home and made a copy of the hard drive as soon as the family left.

On Bruton's computer, detectives discovered several emails where he talked about meeting men and taking them out to a cabin in the woods that he owned, which was about two and a half hours away from Toronto. He claimed that in this cabin, he had a hoist that he used to tie his victims up by their feet to drain their bodies of blood. He would then butcher them, prepare them to cook, cook them, and finally eat them.

These emails were sent to and from men who lived in different countries worldwide and of all ages, from teenagers to retirees. Many of them had included their pictures. In response, Brunton gave them graphically detailed descriptions of how he would kill each of them, how he would prepare them, and cook them before he ate them.

Surprisingly, detectives discovered through these emails that Brunton had paid for some of the men he had chatted with on the *Zambian Meat* website to fly into Toronto to meet him in person. Once even, Brunton drove across the American border to meet a young man, placed him in the trunk of his vehicle, and smuggled him back into Canada. These emails made it imperative that they didn't let Brunton out of their sight or let him meet and be alone with any other men.

Another piece of evidence found on Brunton's computer that police were not expecting were several videos of what looked like a boy's changing room or locker, which they figured to be the hockey arena where he coached a boys team.

They initially decided to hold onto these videos and not arrest him on these charges yet. They wanted to wait and catch him in the act of meeting someone from the *Zambian Meat* website. Or until they had more evidence of Brunton's involvement in the missing men or proof of him killing and eating any of them.

The detective searched Brunton's emails and messages for a long time. They had to go over every detail and locate the men he had communicated with over the *Zambian Meat* website to find out who they were and make sure they were still alive. They also searched to see if Brunton had any connection to the missing gay men. It took police another six months to find the links to the missing men, but they were there. Skanda and Basir were members of gay dating apps such as *Silver Daddies*, and they went to male strip clubs, and Brunton did the same.

Detectives found what looked to be a contract Brunton had signed with a fifteen-year-old boy. In the agreement, Brunton was to kill, butcher, cook, and eat the fifteen-year-old boy. The police faced finding the young man to ensure that Brunton hadn't hurt him. Later, they found the young man living in Colorado, and he was safe.

Detective Coffey then approached Brunton on the *Zambian Meat* website, pretending to be a young 15-year-old boy asking him if he would kill and eat him. The two corresponded for a few weeks until Brunton set up a date where they could go to his cabin. It was to be there where he would kill and eat him. Brunton didn't show up to meet the boy as planned. The police decided it was too dangerous for this to go on. They went to Brunton's home and arrested him for charges relating to his filming the boys he coached while they were in the changing room. They figured that they had spent enough time trying to get any evidence of Brunton's connection to the missing men from Toronto.

At the station, detectives asked him about his connection with the *Zambian Meat* website, which he admitted to being on but said it was a complete fantasy. When they asked him about his descriptions on the website, such as being a butcher, he told them that it was part of role-playing. He said he was never involved in any actual cannibalism.

Moving away from the *Zambian Meat* website and cannibalism, the detectives started questioning him about the missing gay men. They first asked him if he had ever met Skanda or if he knew who he was. He claimed that he had seen Skanda at the strip club he went to but never knew him. When asked about Hamid, Brunton claimed he had known him for about ten years and had had sex with him a few times, but he had never really talked to or knew anything about him.

Detectives then asked him how he knew Luka Magnotta. Brunton denied ever meeting him. Brunton told them that he never believed that there were any cannibals or people who ate human flesh, at least not until Magnotta came along.

Brunton admitted that he hid a teenage boy in his trunk and drove him across the U.S. Canada border. Still, without any physical evidence, police couldn't charge him with anything relating to the boy or to do with cannibalism or being responsible for the missing men.

When first asked, Brunton denied knowing anything about any film with boys in a hockey change room. Detectives then showed him the videos of the teenage boys they got from his computer. Brunton decided he would no longer talk with the police and lawyered up.

Brunton was charged with sixty-six criminal charges for producing child porn, sexual assaults, extortion, kidnapping, and other sexual offenses against minors, centered around him filming the young boys in the change room. He was convicted and only got three years' probation. Police kept a surveillance team on Brunton but knew they were at a dead end.

Just as they looked for links with Brunton,

Detective Josh McKenzie searched through the evidence they had found for all three of the missing victims to see if he could find some connection between them. Some of the links were obvious, but they couldn't rely on them as they were commonalities between many gay people who all lived in Toronto. A few went to the same clubs, coffee shops, and even bathhouses. The three missing men had even dated some of the same guys, so it would be hard to determine which similarities you needed to take seriously.

Then something caught the detective's eye—the email address verfoxx51@hotmail.com. This email address was in Skanda's contact list and also found in Basir's home, written on a pad of paper. When he looked further into the email address owner, he found it belonged to Bruce McArthur.

On September 23, 2013, a warrant was filed stating that an interview was scheduled with Bruce McArthur regarding the disappearances of Skanda Navaratnam and Abdulbasir Faizi. McArthur came in for the interview without hesitation.

During the interview, McArthur told detectives that he knew Skanda, but they never had sex with each other. They were only friends. They would go to the Eagles or other gay clubs and just hang out and talk.

Detectives showed McArthur all the pictures

they had of the missing men from the area to see if he knew any of them. McArthur said that he recognized Hamid and had known him for about ten years. The two had been together sexually before, but nothing was regular, and no relationship evolved. But later, the police found out that Hamid had actually worked for McArthur, helping him do a landscaping project that lasted about a month.

When he looked at Basir's picture, he said he didn't know who he was and had never seen him in the area before. Detectives believed what McArthur told them and let him go.

By April 2014, police decided to close Project Houston. They had no new leads to follow as far as the missing men, and they had completed the file on Brunton.

SOROUSH MAHMUDI 2015

Soroush Mahmudi vanished in August of 2015. His remains were not found until February of 2018, just one month after Bruce McArthur had been charged with several murder charges, including Soroush's.

He was last seen on the corner of Markham Road and Blakemanor Boulevard two years earlier. Mahmudi worked as a professional painter. According to his wife, Fareena Marezook, Soroush got up early that morning, around 4 a.m., to go to work, just as he usually did, and had made breakfast for his step-son just before he left.

Marezook, who came from Sri Lanka, said that her husband was from Iran, and they had met in Canada twelve years earlier. He had three sisters and one brother, who still lived in Iran. Both of his parents had died years before also in Iran. He had no reason to go to the gay village and never knew that he ever did, as the couple lived in an apartment building in the Toronto suburb of Scarborough.

The couple had once lived together in Barrie, Ontario, and had filed for bankruptcy about one year before he went missing in 2014. He had a string of run-ins with the law. They all seemed to involve him driving while impaired by alcohol or driving while his license was suspended. There were even convictions for his failure to appear in court.

There was also one assault conviction on his record, which was from an ex-girlfriend of his. Strangely she told a story of meeting him at the same bar where they were filming the gay television series, *Queer as Folk*. The two dated and eventually moved in together. She claimed that Soroush was attracted to trans women.

He told her that he had to do some terrible things when he lived in Iran. He hid in Turkey because he thought the Iranian Government would punish him for his actions. He claimed that this was the reason for him drinking so much alcohol.

After about three years, he started to get violent with her. When she tried to leave him one day, he hit her over the head with the glass jar from a blender they had in the kitchen. He then began to beat her, and when a neighbor came by to find out what was going on, he ran away.

10

DEAN LISOWICK 2016

Dean Lisowick was born in Winnipeg, Manitoba, and moved with his parents to Toronto. By the time he was eight years old, his parents had split up. The Catholic Children's Aid Society had taken him in, and he was eventually placed in a foster home in the farming town of Udora.

At the foster home, Dean was not the only boy there as they constantly had a steady flow of boys come through the house. Sometimes the boys were adopted, and sometimes they ran away. Some would be arrested for minor, petty crimes and placed in another more strict home or even youth detention.

When Dean was old enough, he left his foster home and moved back to Toronto. He didn't have a plan. He had no place to live or job to go to. He just left.

After Dean's death, it was discovered that he was being abused sexually at his foster home by his foster father, which is probably why he left as soon as he could.

It didn't take long for Dean to become involved in the drug culture and party life that was popular in Toronto in the mid-nineties. He had several drug possession and assault charges. In 1994, after becoming a father, he left his girlfriend and stayed in the Gay Village, knowing he would not be seen there by his girlfriend.

Dean became an escort and went by the name of "Laser." He identified as bisexual.

Dean found it hard to find a legitimate job with a police record of drugs, assault, and prostitution. He had to beg for money on the downtown streets of Toronto. He slept in shelters when he could get a bed and ate at the soup kitchens.

After about ten years of that lifestyle, he decided that he would get sober and stop using drugs. But when he just disappeared, nobody noticed or cared. There were no reports made to the police about him missing. The police didn't have much to go on, even if reports were made. They didn't even have an address at which he lived. He was also a gay drug-addicted male prostitute, which was not a priority for police to find.

11

SELIM ESEN APRIL 2017

Esen was last seen on the night of April 15, 2017, walking on Bloor Street near Ted Rogers Way in Toronto. According to Selim's brother, Omar Esen, he was a very kind-hearted, friendly man who loved to work in the garden.

They were both from Turkey, where Selim was very unhappy and felt unsafe because he was gay. Selim was born in Istanbul, but the two brothers lived in Ankara. While Selim worked to help support his parents, he studied and received his university degree.

At first, Selim moved to Australia, but after deciding to marry his Canadian boyfriend in 2013, he moved there. Eventually, the relationship ended, but Selim stayed living in Toronto.

ANDREW KINSMAN
JUNE 2017

On June 26, 2017, 49-year-old Andrew Kinsman disappeared. He was the manager of the apartment building where he lived in Cabbagetown. He was very popular among his tenants and the gay community, and his work with the People with Aids group in Toronto.

Around the time he disappeared, it was the time of the gay pride parade. People were busy, so nobody was immediately concerned that he was missing. Kinsman also didn't fit the profile of the previous men who had gone missing from the gay community. Not only was he caucasian, but he was also a substantial 240 pounds. After a few days of Kinsman not returning home, it was reported to the police. Friends of his placed missing person posters with his picture around the area.

The first suspect that came to his friend's mind was a man that Kinsman occasionally hooked up with—a man who was also very into the psychology of serial killers. Kinsman was a big fan of true crime, and that's why he and this other man connected.

The police searched Kinsman's apartment and went through his personal computer. There, they found files about the British serial killer named Dennis Nilsen, a serial killer known to have had sex with his victims after they died. This fact would end up being very ironic as McArthur had the same proclivities as Nilsen.

Kinsman was also known to have been into BDSM sex, basically role-playing during sex, and would be into bondage and discipline and also including sadomasochism. The police were stuck on this fact, assuming that anyone involved in this behavior was asking to be hurt or even killed. But the opposite is actually true. The number of people assaulted or seriously injured in this type of activity is very low. Most people in these sexual relationships have pre-play negotiations set up, and safe words are often arranged, which would immediately stop any activity they find uncomfortable.

Within this computer folder, they also found ten photographs of Bruce McArthur, taken with Kinsman's camera on September 11, 2010. Police became suspicious of McArthur when they noticed "Bruce 3 p.m." written on Kinsman's calendar at his home on the same date he went missing, June 26th.

There was no new movement in the case until August, after detectives found some locally placed cameras outside Kinsman's apartment building. After going through the camera footage from locations outside of Kinsman's apartment, detectives found what looked like Kinsman leaving his apartment and getting into a red Dodge Caravan on the 26th just a few minutes after 3 p.m. – just as it was written on Kinsman's calendar.

Police searched the area for more available cameras and found the same van in several other shots. It was at 3:06 p.m., the red van had pulled up outside his apartment building, and you could see what looked like the same-sized man jumping into the passenger side of the vehicle.

Unfortunately, none of the videos caught the caravan's license plate number.

Detective Coffey then went out to a few Dodge dealerships in the area to see if he could find someone who might be able to tell him a little more about the van for which they were looking. Coffey stopped at the fourth Dodge dealership, and one of the managers identified the caravan as the 2004 25th anniversary edition.

With this new information, Coffey obtained a list of all registered owners of the 2004 Dodge Caravans in the province of Ontario from the Department of Motor Vehicles. There was a total of 6,181 in Ontario alone, so they could imagine how many were in the whole country. The caravan could have also been American, so the odds of finding the correct van were very unlikely.

One of the detectives on the case then remembered the name "Bruce" was written on Kinsman's calendar. So, he searched for 2004 Dodge Caravans registered to anyone with the first name of Bruce in the province. This time, they got back much better results. There were only five people named Bruce who owned a 2004 Dodge Caravan. Coffey had to hope that it was, in fact, the Bruce written on Kinsman's calendar on June 26 who picked him up that day that they had caught on the camera.

Coffey started to do background checks on the

five men named Bruce. Only one was on his system, Bruce McArthur. So, he ran McArthur's criminal history. Even though McArthur had been granted a pardon to remove his assault conviction, it was only removed from the general public's access. The police still had access to all the files and knew of his arrest in 2001. But they discovered something even more recent— McArthur had been arrested in 2016 for a different assault case.

It happened in the early evening of June 2016, when McArthur was to meet with an acquaintance, or what they call a "friend-with-benefits" in the community. The two occasionally met up and had sex, probably about five or six times a year, and had done this for several years.

The man he was doing this with was a man who was living 'in the closet,' and they had to meet without letting anybody know. He was probably married and had kids. This friend-with-benefits situation was an advantage to many gay men who liked to be involved with married men. They knew there were limits on how much would be expected of them. They never had to worry about having any expectations from the married men.

The two usually met at a Tim Horton's parking lot, where they would have sex in one of their vehicles. That night it would be McArthur's van as it had more room. At first, it started like every other time they met. They started kissing and feeling each other's bodies. It slowly started to get a little rough, which was something they both liked. Only this time, McArthur started to choke out his partner violently. The man began to fight back, and eventually, the rough play broke up. The man jumped out of the van and called 911 from his cell phone. McArthur got scared, jumped into the driver's seat, and drove away.

Two patrol officers approached the scene and talked to the shaky man. Unfortunately, this man and McArthur had never exchanged their real names, so he didn't know who he was, but he could give them McArthur's cell number. From that, police could locate his address and go to McArthur's apartment.

While this was happening, McArthur did what he did after his first attack in 2001. He went to the police station to confess his crime. He walked up to the front desk and told the officer that he wanted to make a statement and tell his side of the story. Soon, Sergeant Paul Gauthier came from his office, placed McArthur under arrest for suspicion of domestic assault, and walked him into the interrogation room for questioning.

13

BRUCE MCARTHUR'S INTERROGATION

The following is a transcript of Bruce McArthur's interrogation on Monday, June 20, 2016, at 10:17 p.m.

Detective Paul Gauthier: "Okay, sir, so um, just before we begin here, I just want to let you know that we are uh being audio and video recorded right now because there's a camera just up in the corner and uh, this device appears is a microphone, so it's picking up everything that we say, okay?"

Bruce McArthur: "Okay."

Detective Paul Gauthier: "Um, the time right now is uh 10:17 p.m., and today's date is uh Monday, June 20, 2016. My name is Detective Paul Gauthier, G-A-U-T-H-I-E-R, badge number 5371 of 32 division. My partner here is…"

Constable Dying: "Constable Dying, uh 10055, 32 division."

Detective Paul Gauthier: "Okay, sir, and your name is?"

Bruce McArthur: "Bruce McArthur."

Detective Paul Gauthier: "And if you could spell it for me, please?"

Bruce McArthur: "Uh, B-R-U-C-E, and McArthur, M, small "c" capital "A", R-T-H-U-R."

Detective Paul Gauthier: "Okay, Sir, and uh, right now uh, you're under arrest. Uh, you're placed under arrest this evening for the offense of assault, okay. Uh, you've been brought here, to 32 division for the purposes of being investigated, uh, for that offense, okay. So, a few minutes ago, we just had a brief conversation, and I introduced myself, and I gave you an opportunity to provide a statement, and you said that you wanted to do so, is that correct?"

Bruce McArthur: "That's correct."

Detective Gauthier: "Okay, and at the same time, I also asked you if you wanted to speak to a lawyer before doing so, and I'm going to ask you again. Do you wish to do that before we begin?"

Bruce McArthur: "No, that's fine."

Detective Gauthier: "Okay, Sir. Um, so an allegation has been made against you, and this officer, in just a moment, is going to let you know exactly what that allegation is okay. What I'm going to do to you right now is just read your caution and let you know, um, that you're being investigated for the offense of assault, okay. You're not obliged to say anything unless you wish to do so, but whatever you say may be given in evidence. Do you understand?"

Bruce McArthur: "I do."

Detective Gauthier: "Okay, do you wish to say anything and answer the charge?"

Bruce McArthur: *mumbles something unrecognizable*

Detective Paul Gauthier: "Again, do you wish to provide us a statement?"

Bruce McArthur: "Yes"

Detective Paul Gauthier: "Some clarity as to what happened."

Bruce McArthur: "Yes."

Detective Paul Gauthier: "Okay, so to understand, Sir, again, you're not under any obligation to give us the statement whatsoever. You're allowed to uh cease uh communicating with us at any time, but we're certainly giving you an opportunity to present your side of the story, Sir. So, this officer is just going to give you an overview here of what's being alleged, okay?"

Constable Dying: "The allegations are that around 6:30 p.m. this evening, you met up with a gentleman by the name of (bleeped out), um, at the intersection of Bathurst and Finch. During the course of your involvement with him, there was an allegation made of an assault which in choking was the allegation made, and that's basically why you're under arrest today for that assault, okay?"

Bruce McArthur: "Okay"

Detective Paul Gauthier: "So, sir, if you would like to provide us with your account of what occurred earlier this evening."

Bruce McArthur: "Well, I met (bleeped out), and we talked about going for dinner, but he said he needed to take a shower, so I said I'd meet him at the Tim Horton's Finch and Bathurst. And so, he arrived, and we were going to have sex, and he suggested doing the back of his truck since it hadn't been used yet. It was a brand new truck. I said, well, there's more room in the back of my van. So, we went to my van. Um, and we started um kissing, and I put my hand down his pants, and he wanted me to squeeze his penis, but then he said he wanted it more challenging and to pinch it, to pinch and pinch and pinch just as hard as I could.

So, I did, and he got aroused by that. So, I thought, okay, so he likes it rough. So, I put my hand to his throat and just for a few seconds. Because, before that, he's firm, he just completely turned around and grabbed me by the throat he said. He said, now, I'm going to show you what I'm going to do to you. And he kept me about the throat to the point that I couldn't breathe. So, I put my hands up in the air like surrender because I couldn't talk, and that's when he finally let go.

And then he jumped out of the car, and he said, I don't want to see you again. So, I sat there because I was kind of out of breath, and I thought he was getting his car to leave because he started the car and it was running. I could hear it running because he was parked beside me, and the next thing I heard him say was the 9-1-1 or whatever. So, I thought, oh gosh, he's calling the police officers, and so, um, I got out. And then he got out and walked around and was taking my license plate and that. And so, um, that's when I got kind of nervous like kind of currently drove off.

And then the more I thought about it, I felt I should go and get my side, but I could not think of where the police station was in that area. So, the only one I could think of was downtown. But then I realized there's one somewhere in Eglinton, and that's where I drove to."

Detective Paul Gauthier: "Just on the last point, sir, um, did you go to that police station on Eglinton before, um, the officers contacted you?"

Bruce McArthur: "Yeah, no, I went there, and then they came to me."

Detective Paul Gauthier: "Okay."

Bruce McArthur: "The lady I spoke to told me that I came to make a statement. She said she ran my name, and nothing appeared on the screen. I said well, what about my license plate, and she said it would show up too. So, that's when she called."

Detective Paul Gauthier: "So you went of your own free will. It's not like an officer called you to come to see…."

Bruce McArthur: "No one called me."

Detective Paul Gauthier: "Excuse me, anything like that, yes, okay. Um, so you indicated that this incident occurred with (bleeped out) uh what's his last name?"

Bruce McArthur: "I don't know his last name."

Detective Paul Gauthier: "And how long have you known him?"

Bruce McArthur: "Two or three years maybe."

Detective Paul Gauthier: "Okay, and as you're describing it, um, this is somebody you're in an intimate relationship with, is that right?"

Bruce McArthur: "Well, no, intimate, we see maybe, I see him maybe two-three months, maybe."

Detective Paul Gauthier: "Okay, and how did the two of you meet?"

Bruce McArthur: "Online, I think."

Detective Paul Gauthier: "Okay, has anything like this ever happened before where things got out of hand?"

Bruce McArthur: "Not like that. No, not that quickly or not, you know, just like that."

Detective Paul Gauthier: "Things have never gotten violent?"

Bruce McArthur: "No, no."

Detective Paul Gauthier: "Okay, um, so you indicated that you think it was around 6:30 p.m., you said?"

Bruce McArthur: "Yeah, between 6:30 and seven."

Detective Paul Gauthier: "Okay, you said you think the...."

Bruce McArthur: "Yeah, something like that, I think, would be 6:30 or seven, yes."

Detective Paul Gauthier: "Okay, and you said you met at the Tim Horton's parking lot at Bathurst and Finch, is that right?"

Bruce McArthur: "Yeah."

Detective Paul Gauthier: "Okay, so it still would have been bright outside at 6:30, right?"

Bruce McArthur: "Yes."

Detective Paul Gauthier: "Okay, and you indicated that you were going to have sex in his truck, but it was new."

Bruce McArthur: "He suggested that, and I said, well, there's more room in the back of my van than in your truck."

Detective Paul Gauthier: "Okay, what kind of truck did he have?"

Bruce McArthur: "A Ford. Um, a Ford, something four doors."

Detective Paul Gauthier: "Okay. Your van is, you know what, it's a Dodge Caravan?"

Bruce McArthur: "Dodge Caravan."

Detective Paul Gauthier: "Okay, and you said the two you were parked beside each other, right?"

Bruce McArthur: "Yeah."

Detective Paul Gauthier: "And then you went into your van, is that right, and then you said you started kissing?"

Bruce McArthur: "Yeah."

Detective Paul Gauthier: "And that's when this incident happened, is that right?"

Bruce McArthur: "Well, then when my hand went down his pants, and he said squeeze, pinch it as hard as you can."

Detective Paul Gauthier: "Okay, um, what part of the van were you in when this happened?"

Bruce McArthur: "Let's see the back seat."

Detective Paul Gauthier: "Like the back seat are like the very back of...."

Bruce McArthur: "Well, there's only one seat. The seats are all except for one seat, one bucket seat in there."

Detective Paul Gauthier: "Okay. And was there a possibility for anybody else to see what had gone on?"

Bruce McArthur: "Yes."

Detective Paul Gauthier: "Okay, why do you say that?"

Bruce McArthur: "Well, because you're lying on the floor, who could see you?"

Detective Paul Gauthier: "Oh, so you're down some?"

Bruce McArthur: "Yeah, we're lying flat on the floor."

Detective Paul Gauthier: "Okay, and you indicated that you started to pinch his penis, and he indicated that he wanted it uh, rougher, I believe?"

Bruce McArthur: "He said harder, hit it as hard as you can do it."

Detective Paul Gauthier: "Okay, and at that point, you said you motioned your hands up to his neck."

Bruce McArthur: "Well after, you know, we did that for a while until he was getting harder and harder."

Detective Paul Gauthier: "Okay, okay."

Bruce McArthur: "So, I figured he liked that."

Detective Paul Gauthier: "Okay, what was your, um, reason for bringing your hands up to his neck? What was your understanding?"

Bruce McArthur: "I think I thought he liked it rough."

Detective Paul Gauthier: "Okay."

Bruce McArthur: "He was getting off on that."

Detective Paul Gauthier: "And then you indicated that immediately he put his hands around your neck, is that right?"

Bruce McArthur: "He quickly, he was like, he's firm and before you know it he just had completely swung around and was facing me on pushing me down, and his hands were around my neck."

Detective Paul Gauthier: "Okay."

Bruce McArthur: "Like, like really quick."

Detective Paul Gauthier: "So, there's a brief struggle?"

Bruce McArthur: "Yeah. Well, that, well, I couldn't struggle with him after.

Once he had his hands around my neck, he was solid."

Detective Paul Gauthier: "Okay, um, how long did this last for approximately?"

Bruce McArthur: "Seconds."

Detective Paul Gauthier: "Are you injured at all, sir?"

Bruce McArthur: "No."

Detective Paul Gauthier: "Do you believe he would have been injured?"

Bruce McArthur: "I didn't think so."

Detective Paul Gauthier: "Lacey, do you have any questions?"

Constable: "No, that's pretty good."

Detective Paul Gauthier: "Okay, sir, just before we conclude, is there anything else you feel might be important to tell us before we end the interview?"

Bruce McArthur: "Like what?"

Detective Paul Gauthier: "I don't know what else. We always give people an opportunity to say something we may haven't asked before we conclude."

Bruce McArthur: "I don't know. We've had sex, you know, numerous times, and I never had a problem."

Detective Paul Gauthier: "Sure, okay, all right uh, time that I have is uh, 10:28, and we can complete the interview here."

AFTERMATH

AT THE TIME of this interview, McArthur had already killed six men. And after this interview, he killed two more. About two years after Gauthier conducted this interview, it came into the spotlight after McArthur's arrest. The public was asking why Gauthier let McArthur go so soon.

It wasn't long before the media caught wind of the interrogation from 2016 for a different assault case and started printing the details. It wasn't long before Toronto Police Department felt enough pressure to charge Officer Gauthier with neglect of duty and insubordination and held a disciplinary tribunal to find out what happened. The tribunal was on May 21, 2021, and Gauthier pleaded not guilty to the charges.

Gauthier released McArthur with no charges even after knowing he had tried to strangle another man during a sexual encounter because he believed the man wanted it rough. The police prosecutor told the tribunal that the investigation of McArthur for the assault was flawed. Prosecutors Alexandra Ciobotaru and Mattison Chinneck also told the court that Detective Gauthier's investigation fell far short of what the Toronto Police's domestic violence policy expected. They left the court wondering why Gauthier didn't conduct a thorough investigation. "He had a one-sided, tunnel vision view of the investigation."

Chinneck asked, "How can you release someone with no charges? Someone who tried to strangle his intimate partner to death without even having spoken to the victim?" Another point the prosecutors brought up was why Gauthier failed to get a video recording of the victim's statement or even to follow up with the victim himself. He only took the victim's statement and wrote it in a memo pad, which was written verbatim from another officer's account of the assault.

Chinneck also complained about Gauthier's

performance in his interrogation of McArthur. "He only spent nine minutes interviewing McArthur with relevant questions. And it's hard to imagine how a thorough investigation can be conducted in that time."

There were more failings in this investigation, including police not taking any photos of the victim or his injuries from the assault. All of this shows that he didn't even complete the basics of a domestic assault investigation.

Gauthier retired. His lawyer, Lawrence Gridin, described the whole case against his client as politically motivated because as the list of McArthur's victims got more prominent, the criticism of the Toronto Police Department got more significant and more extreme. Therefore, Gauthier was just the scapegoat or officer to throw under the bus.

Gridin explained that in February of 2018, Toronto Police Chief Mark Saunders was interviewed for the *Globe and Mail*, where he said McArthur had slipped through the cracks and not been noticed by the detectives because the public didn't give police any tips on the case. That same week, Saunders faced much criticism from both the media and the public. He argued Saunders was under so much pressure at the time that his client made the perfect scapegoat for him.

There were two specific parts of Gauthier's investigation that the public didn't understand or like. The first was that the detective didn't need to take after-the-fact photos of injuries or get a videotaped statement for the victim. During testimony from different police officers, they claimed that videotaped interviews were the best, but 99 percent of the time, they just used a memo pad.

"This hearing cannot be about whether Gauthier should have pressed charges on McArthur, but about whether he followed the standard procedure of the police department," Gridin claimed. "Even though the public didn't like this procedure, it wouldn't be proper to discipline just one officer, Gauthier, for using it, as most of the officers there did the same thing during a domestic assault case. Based on the circumstances of this specific case, there wasn't enough evidence to hold McArthur or charge him, so it was reasonable to release him," Gridin continued. "Lacking subjective grounds to believe McArthur committed a crime, there was only one way this could go: to let him go. It's that simple," Gridin finished.

During an independent review of the Toronto Police Department's handling of the McArthur case, they found that it was because of investigative flaws that detectives didn't have the opportunity to stop McArthur sooner than they should have to stop his killing spree.

The Ontario Court Judge Gloria Epstein reviewed Gauthier's investigation of McArthur for the domestic assault and stated that Gauthier releasing McArthur was premature at best. Epstein also thought it was well arguable that the evidence did not support letting McArthur go because there was nothing to suggest the victim had consented to be choked. She also wanted to know why Gauthier didn't choose to speak to the victim of the assault during his investigation. The court rested and would decide later. If Gauthier was found guilty of misconduct, he could face penalties such as dismissal. Even though, in this case, the prosecution was not asking for that.

About three months later, on August 22, 2021, the court returned with its decision. Gauthier was not found guilty of professional conduct, which had the expected reactions. Gridin, Gauthier's attorney, said it was a vindication of his client, while McArthur's victims' families were disheartened.

The court wrote, "While I would have preferred further steps to be taken, nothing has been presented to demonstrate, to any degree of certainty, that had those steps been taken, Sergeant Gauthier could have formed reasonable grounds to arrest McArthur in 2016. But Gauthier cannot be found guilty of violating a mandatory order if the order was not mandatory."

The procedure was not well written regarding domestic assaults and the steps required by law enforcement. The policy should be updated so mistakes like those in the McArthur case wouldn't happen.

Now, if Gauthier had taken the time to interview the victim to find out what he claimed happened, perhaps he would have thought differently about charging McArthur with assault. And from there, investigating him further.

The victim stated, "I've got to get out of this van was all I could think of while he was holding me down and choking me. He could hear the cars driving by outside of the van but had no way to scream out. It was a busy intersection with lots of walking traffic, but there would be no way of seeing them through McArthur's darkened van windows."

The two men met in 2011 on a gay dating app just for a sexual hook-up. The victim was living a straight life with his family, friends, and work, so he didn't want a relationship and wanted to keep things secretive. He had the urge to have romantic connections with other men but didn't want to go to public places such as gay bars to meet them. He had a fear of being caught.

This was and is not an unusual thing within the gay community. In some cases, gay men like this type of relationship as the married or straight man who is hidden but wants to meet up has boundaries. They don't have to worry about it becoming a serious relationship or having to commit.

Their very first meet-up was good for both of them, so they decided that they would do it again. They met periodically for sexual relations and nothing more. McArthur had always seemed like a very nice man to the victim over the years and showed no signs of violence.

The first time the victim got any weird feelings about McArthur was when he was invited over to a house that McArthur was taking care of for friends while they were on vacation. McArthur cooked him a nice dinner, and the evening went well until he asked him to put on an old ratty-looking fur coat so he could take photos of him in the skin. The victim felt awkward as he didn't want to wear a fur coat, especially an older, dirty one. McArthur kept pushing him to do it, and even though he thought it was weird, he eventually put on the coat and let McArthur take pictures of him. He had no feelings about ever wanting to wear any women's clothing.

That same fur coat was lying on the floor of McArthur's van that night when he met with him at the Tim Horton's parking lot to have sex. At first, he didn't think much of it and thought perhaps it was just there so that they wouldn't get dirty from the floor in the van. McArthur removed all the back seats, so there was only a bare, greasy floor on which to lay.

Earlier that day, McArthur had called him from a pay phone to set up their meeting. This was unusual as they had each other's cell phone numbers and usually would text each other when one of them was in the mood or had time to meet. Then, when the victim arrived home that day from work, McArthur was waiting outside in his apartment building parking lot. Shocked, he told McArthur that he needed to go in and shower first and that he could meet him somewhere. McArthur suggested the Tim Hortons on the corner of Bathurst and Finch.

After the victim arrived at the meeting place, he got out of his vehicle, and McArthur insisted that they get into the back of his van because it had more room to play around. The van was parked at the far end of the parking lot, facing a subdivision of houses. It wasn't exactly the most private place, but because McArthur had tinted his van windows, nobody would be able to see inside.

After they got into the van, the two men laid down with McArthur lying behind him.

McArthur slowly moved the man's right arm behind his back, then reached over with his hand and started to press down on his throat, making it so that he couldn't breathe properly. At first, the victim said he was confused. He turned his head all he could and looked into McArthur's eyes. Right away, he could tell that McArthur was going to kill him. "He had a look of determination and anger."

The man struggled and moved around as much as he could, but McArthur had his whole body weight on top of him and wrapped his legs around his. After fighting with McArthur for a few minutes, he broke free from his grip. He was so afraid that he just burst out of the van to escape McArthur. He then turned to McArthur and yelled at him that he would call the police.

The man ran back to his vehicle, dialed the police from his cell phone, and told the dispatcher that a man had just tried to strangle him. His in-car camera caught McArthur driving away from the scene in his van. The man immediately started his vehicle and started chasing McArthur while still being on the phone with the police dispatcher. He chased McArthur for a short while until the dispatcher convinced him to pull over, stop, and let them catch the man who tried to strangle him.

The man waited until both police and an ambulance arrived at where he was waiting. The officer took his statement. Meanwhile, McArthur had the idea to go to the police station and report what had happened, just as he had done in 2001. He got away with it then, so he figured he might get away with it again.

14

PROJECT PRISM JULY 2017

The police launched Project Prism on July 28, 2017, to investigate the missing gay men in Toronto. Detectives announced in a press conference that the focus was on the two missing gay men from the Toronto Gay Village—Andrew Kinsman and Selim Esen. Though Andrew Kinsman didn't quite fit the profile of the other missing men, he was included in the investigation. Detective Sergeant Michael Richmond was assigned to oversee the project, and to lead the studies was Detective Sergeant Hank Idsinga. Idsinga had been on the homicide squad in Toronto for over thirteen years and was given six uniformed officers from the street police squad in Toronto and one officer from the sex crimes unit.

The project first had to understand that all the

missing persons or victims used online apps to meet each other – not in person, in a bar, or in a coffee shop. Online was a new lifestyle in which people met. The police would have to learn how these apps worked to investigate this new way of connecting with people the victims didn't know.

Idsinga would later say that the project started because of the evidence they found in Kinsman's apartment. Kinsman's missing status was reported within three days of his disappearance, which was different from the other missing people in the area. Another difference was Kinsman's appearance and stature. He was a 6 foot 4 and over 250-pound caucasian man, well known in the community because of his work as an apartment building manager who volunteered for different charity groups. He wasn't like the others who had been reported missing—they mainly led a more transient lifestyle.

Some local camera footage showed what looked like Kinsman getting into McArthur's vehicle on the same date and time that the name "Bruce" was written on Kinsman's calendar in his apartment. Because of this clue, the police had the place where Kinsman went missing and the date. So, they could start going through any cameras recording in the area of his apartment building, which led to finding the suspect.

After placing their new suspect, Bruce

McArthur, under surveillance, police learned that he sold his Dodge Caravan in September. When they went to the dealership that now owned his caravan, they took it in their possession and examined it for any clues. The lab ended up finding traces of blood that matched that of the missing Kinsman.

Later in November, police cadaver dogs started searching for bodies, starting with where McArthur lived and worked. The dogs didn't indicate human remains at the residence where McArthur kept all his landscaping work tools and lawnmowers, but police set up cameras to watch him.

Soon after this, more DNA results came back from McArthur's caravan. This time, they matched the missing person Esen's DNA. From that, they entered McArthur's apartment without him knowing it and made a copy of his computer's hard drive. Finding the DNA gave detectives enough evidence to obtain a search warrant for McArthur's apartment and his electronic devices and computers.

One key element that detectives mentioned was that they thought of Esen as a transient person as he always had a silver travel case with wheels, so they suspected he didn't have a permanent address. He also struggled with drug use, a commonality for missing gay men.

Project Prism started a wave of fear throughout the community. Any doubt that had been in people's minds quickly vanished as now the police were investigating. There were now at least five gay men missing with no explanations.

Everyone in the neighborhood believed there was some connection between these men. Police released a statement warning everyone in the gay village that they should take extreme caution using any dating apps and to use extreme caution when meeting someone they had met on one of these apps.

In most of the gay community, the talk was that there was a serial killer out there of gay men. Still, police were publicly downplaying this by saying there was no evidence of any relationship between the missing men. There was a significant distrust of the police. Not that people believed the police were part of any conspiracy or involved in the actual disappearance, but it was more a feeling that the police were not interested in missing gay men. It seemed that they didn't care about these men and placed them on a lower priority, along with drug addicts.

15

KIRUSHUNA KUMAR KANAGARATNAM SEPT. 2017

Kirushuna Kumar Kanagaratnam fled his homeland Sri Lanka after the civil war broke out in the summer of 2010. He was one of over 100 people on a ship that escaped from their war-torn country, searching for a place of refuge. Kanagaratnam applied for asylum but was turned down and ordered to leave the country, but he never did.

After being turned away from Australia, the ship headed for Canada, the harbour in Vancouver. He decided to stay in Canada and go into hiding. He couldn't possibly go back to Sri Lanka as the war raged on. It destroyed the schools and ended life as he knew it. In 2007, his older brother was shot to death. He didn't tell his family about being deported as he didn't want to put them through any more pain and worry. So, he worked his way to Toronto, where he found some of his distant family members and worked jobs that paid cash and were off the record. He mainly worked labor jobs like shoveling driveways, landscaping, or construction. He made enough money to send home, about $500 every month.

Suddenly the money stopped coming home, and his family no longer heard from him. They were worried that maybe he was into trouble or perhaps the government was going to deport him. They knew they couldn't file a missing person report as he could be in hiding and thought it would be better not to let the police know that he was even in the country.

Only today, there was something new that the press didn't expect. On March 15, 2018, Detective Sergeant Hank Idsinga held a press conference to update where the police were in their investigation into the murders and victims of Bruce McArthur. Idsinga was going to release a photo of a man who they believed was another victim of McArthur's. They had used all their resources and needed the public's help to try and identify the man.

The picture Idsinga showed was shockingly odd—his eyes were almost completely closed, even like he was asleep. He had tangled, messed-up hair and a beard that looked like he had not washed or looked after in a long while. His face and head were unnatural, almost like he had been drugged or asleep when they took the photo.

Idsinga warned the media that when they broadcast this man's picture that a family member may see this picture and not realize that he was dead. Also, he told them there would be no information on how the police came into possession of this picture.

Throughout the next few weeks, police called all missing person's families to see if they had seen the newly released photo or if they had a picture of their missing loved one when they had a beard. The photo release added more stress to the community and tension between them and the police. Everyone with a lost friend or family member was on edge as it was unknown whether they were a victim of McArthur or not. If anybody wondered if there were more victims, they knew now that there were.

On April 16th, Idsinga held another press conference, announcing that they had discovered the deceased man's identity in the photo. It was Kirushna Kumar Kanagaratnam. The police believed he was murdered sometime between September 3rd to December 14, 2015. His family members, who spoke English and got the news from the police, decided not to tell their parents the truth behind his death. Instead, they said he had died in a car crash.

PART III

JUDGMENT DAY

16

THE ARREST OF MCARTHUR

Around mid-January the following year, 2018, the forensic analysis of McArthur's home computer started showing some results. His deleted files were photos of his victims in different poses and positions. He took them after they were dead. After this find, detectives put out an order that McArthur would not be alone with any other possible victim. They were ordered to arrest him immediately if found in such a circumstance.

The situation happened shortly after that when McArthur took a man to his apartment on January 18, 2018. The police arrested him that day. When they entered his apartment, the man was tied to his bed but not injured. This man had come from the middle east just five years prior and was a closeted gay man who was still married.

The two men had met through dating apps and had sex a few times. Just before police had arrived, McArthur had handcuffed the man to his bed and gagged his mouth. He had just placed a plastic bag over the man's head when the police knocked on his door.

Now that they had arrested McArthur, Detective Idsinga and the police, believing that he had killed others, had to act quickly to identify victims. They knew that McArthur was a serial killer, and now they had to go back in time and find out where his reign of terror began. The investigation included contacting all the other police departments around the country. Hundreds of missing person reports and unsolved death cases would have to be reviewed to see if there was any connection to McArthur.

Meanwhile, the police had to thoroughly search all the properties where McArthur had lived, stored equipment, or worked. As a landscaper, he had complete access to his customer's lands and properties. He could quickly be digging and moving dirt around each of their properties. Over thirty properties would have to be searched using the resources of the Ontario Forensic Pathologists, Centre for Forensic Sciences, and hundred Ontario Police officers.

On January 18th, police issued five property search warrants. Four were located in Toronto,

THE ARREST OF MCARTHUR | 117

and one in Madoc, Ontario, about 120 miles northeast of the city. McArthur had worked on each of these properties for his landscaping business. The land in Madoc and one of the properties in Toronto were owned by another landscaper who worked with McArthur. Another of the properties in Toronto belonged to one of his ex-boyfriends. These properties ended up being clear of any bodies.

The focus of detectives would be on McArthur's high-rise apartment and the Leaside property, where he kept his work equipment. The police told the owners of the Leaside home to leave and told them they couldn't return until the investigation was completed.

During the property search, the cadaver dogs indicated something was in the planter boxes on the property. Since it was the middle of January, the planters were frozen to the ground. So, the police brought in large heaters to thaw them out to remove them. Then, they were brought to the coroner's office in Toronto. On January 29th, the tests confirmed that police had the skeletal remains of at least three people, who were dismembered and placed in two of the large planter boxes from the property.

When police announced their findings, the bodies were unidentified. But they added three new first-degree murder charges to McArthur, believing they had enough evidence to prosecute him. The detectives presumed that the three bodies belonged to Majeed Kayhan, Soroush Mahmudi, and Dean Lisowick.

The detectives were considerably concerned that there were more victims. As with most serial killers, it starts when they are younger than McArthur was. Their crimes usually begin in their twenties, so this could go back years, and he could be the cause of many more deaths. McArthur was a sales rep for the province of Ontario, so he was constantly on the road going from city to city, so the search would also have to cover a large territory. As it stood, McArthur was already the most prolific serial killer of gays in Canada's history.

One week later, on February 8th, the police announced that they found three more bodies at the Leaside property. They were also in the planters. They positively identified one of the remains of Andrew Kinsman from his fingerprints.

Several more planters were removed from properties throughout the Toronto area. It took police longer to identify the planters with human remains because things were so cold and frozen at that time of the year. The cold made it hard for cadaver dogs to catch a scent, so they had to use large heaters on the properties to thaw out the planters enough to investigate them properly.

The search of McArthur's apartment was the largest in Toronto police history. It took ten forensic officers four months to take over 18,000 photos and remove 1800 pieces of evidence from his bedroom alone. The examination had to be precise as it was thought McArthur had been killing in that apartment for eight years.

By February 23rd, McArthur was charged with six first-degree charges of murder. Skandaraj "Skanda" Navaratnam and Soroush Mahmudi were both positively identified by their dental records.

By early March, the police decided to ask for the public's help and released photos of the unidentified victims hoping they could get some information about them. Their gamble paid off as they received over 500 tips from the phots they released, leading to 22 more possible identities. About the same time, the police said they found another person's remains at the Leaside property.

On April 11th, the police charged McArthur with his seventh first-degree murder for the death of Abdulbasir "Basir" Faizi after his remains were identified. Basir was also found in a planter at the Leaside residence. The police at this time still had an unidentified victim's remains from Leaside, but so far, at all other properties, no bodies were found.

By April 16th, they identified the eighth victim from the Leaside planters as Kirushna Kumar Kanagaratnam, an asylum seeker from Tamil who had not been reported missing. He was probably in hiding as he had been denied by immigration and was under a deportation order. When police investigated Kanagaratnam, they found out that his family had last seen him in August of 2015 and believed that he was murdered sometime in the fall of that same year. McArthur was charged with his eighth first-degree murder charge now.

BY THE END of February 2018, the investigation had to expand outside of the country as McArthur had traveled and taken several vacations outside of Canada. Detectives connected with authorities worldwide, knowing that an investigation like this could take years and cost a substantial amount of money. A major reason for the amount of time it took to investigate this case was that McArthur targeted men who were homeless or very transient. He also used pay phones and avoided public places and streets with cameras.

IN CANADA ALONE, over 600 cold cases or unsolved murders were re-evaluated to see if there were any connections to McArthur. Out of these, 600 police came up with 15 possible matches that took place between 1975 and 1997. Included in these 15 murders were the unsolved murders that occurred there between 1975-1978. The savage murders of that time are reviewed in the chapter titled Gay Village Murders 1975-1978.

McArthur would have been in his early to mid-twenties at the time.

17

TRIAL & SENTENCING

On Tuesday, January 20, 2019, sixty-seven-year-old Bruce McArthur was dressed in a plaid collared shirt and black sweater in a crowded downtown Toronto courthouse. With a blank, hollow, and tired expression, he pleaded guilty to eight first-degree murder charges. After the agreed statement of facts was read out in the Ontario supreme Courthouse, McArthur admitted that he had intended to kill all eight men. Then, all eight men were dismembered so he wouldn't be caught.

McArthur then told the court that with six of his victims, the murder was sexual. He had used ligatures in five of the murders and had confined two of them. McArthur then stated that he was foregoing his right to a trial and pleading guilty voluntarily.

The crown produced several pieces of evidence which tied McArthur to the victims. He had kept some of his victims' belongings in his apartment. The court saw a notebook that belonged to Esen, jewelry that belonged to Lisowick, and a bracelet that Navaratnam owned.

McArthur's guilty plea in court was just over a year after police arrested him on two counts of first-degree murder. During that year, detectives found enough evidence, including the DNA belonging to Esen, Kinsman, Mahmudi, and Navaratnam. McArthur's victims were between the ages of 37 and 58. Six of them were of Middle Eastern or South Asian descent.

Sentencing began on February 4, 2019, and lasted four days. On Friday, February 8, 2019, McArthur was sentenced by the court to life with no chance of parole for twenty-five years. Given his advanced age of 67, McArthur wouldn't be eligible to apply for parole until he was 92. His pleading guilty spared the victims' families a long, nightmarish trial.

The court landed on the side of McArthur's defense attorney, who requested that the client only have to wait twenty-five years before possible parole, while the prosecutor had been asking for fifty years. The court made that decision because if they went with what the prosecution wanted,

McArthur wouldn't be able to apply for parole until he was 116 years old, which was beyond the natural lifespan. The Judge believed that if he imposed the 59-year minimum, it wouldn't be an objective sentence. He added that if McArthur had been a younger man, he would have no problem imposing the longer sentencing terms.

It took the court over an hour to read its final decision, describing McArthur as a sexual predator motivated by a warped, sick gratification to lure vulnerable men to their deaths under the pretense of consensual sex.

He repeatedly strangled his victims and photographed them naked after their deaths, shaving their heads, placing unlit cigars in their mouths, and even dressing some of them in a fur coat and a hat. But even worse, after each of the men's deaths, he subjected them to the greatest post-mortem indignity possible by cutting their bodies into pieces and burying their remains in a plant pot on other people's properties.

"The ability to decapitate and dismember his victims, and do it repeatedly, is pure evil," the Judge read out. McArthur also victimized the dead men's families twice over, first when their loved ones had gone missing and second when they finally learned the horror of what had happened.

The end of the criminal case and sentencing will not bring any more closure to the victims' family loss, and they will have to live with it for the rest of their lives.

PART IV

B-SIDE AND RARETIES

18

GAY VILLAGE MURDERS
1975-1978

Over 40 years ago, fourteen gay men were murdered, and seven of those cases are still unsolved. The unsolved status of those cases was why detectives reviewed and cross-checked to see if McArthur had anything to do with them. After all, he worked only a few blocks from where they were last seen, at the Eaton's department store. Now that McArthur was a known gay serial killer.

In the case of the missing persons involving the gay community and McArthur, police didn't link the murdered men together to look for one serial killer. But could McArthur have committed some of those murders in the 1970s, stopped killing for almost forty years, and started back up again?

It wasn't that long ago, but you still had to

hide being gay in the 1960s and '70s. It was not against the law, so you wouldn't get arrested. But there had been so many years of negative feelings towards gay people in the general public that you didn't want anybody to know you were gay. It would still interfere with you getting a job or even how others treated you when you were at work. Psychiatrists still thought that gay people had an illness that needed to be cured. Even if you figured about half the people believed this, you would be scared, or at the very least, cautious of who you would let know. There were absolutely no human rights involving gay people.

An excellent example would be if you lived in an apartment building and it got out that you were gay, probably having other men over to have gay sex, half of the people in the building would think that you were some pervert doing bad things. They didn't want you living in their structure, especially if they had children. Of course, back then, the mindset was that if you were gay, you must be having deviant sex. Or, they would lump you in with pedophiles and rapists. Your landlord probably wouldn't be happy with you either. Even if they sympathized with you, you would get kicked out of your apartment. There was no place to go with a complaint —nowhere to appeal your case.

That being the general population's mindset, it

only got worse when you look at law enforcement. Police walked the streets and dealt with the communities in person back then, much more than they do now. Often, gay people would have to go to bars hidden from the streets, usually in a back alley and hidden down a dark set of stairs in what looked like a rundown building. Police often would raid those bars, beat up gays, and arrest them for being disorderly. This practice had been going on through the 60s when it was still illegal, so gay men would just have to take it.

The Stonewall Riots were the start of the fight back by gays. It was only a few years after it became legal to be gay, but many of the same officers who had raided, arrested, and beat gay men were still on the force, and just because it wasn't illegal anymore couldn't change how they felt instantly.

When gay men started going missing and turning up dead in the 1970s, the tension between police and the gay community grew. People became scared, and the talk around town was that there was a gay serial killer or perhaps a group of people out to get gay men. Police would deny this and even patronize gay people who complained.

THE GAY VILLAGE MURDERS

1. **Arthur Harold Walkley**, a fifty-one-year-old lecturer at the University of Toronto, was found naked and dead at his apartment at 286 Broden Street on **February 18, 1975**. Police received an emergency phone call at 3:43 a.m. from a man  who refused to give them his name. The call was later traced and came from a pay phone about six blocks from Walkley's apartment building. When an officer arrived at the home, it was locked up tight, and no noises were coming from the house, so the officer left. The owner of the place where Walkley rented his room came home in the morning and found his dead body lying on the front floor. Walkley had been stabbed five times in his chest and back, and his wallet was taken. Police assumed that it was a robbery that went bad. The police investigation that followed showed that Walkley was at a gay tavern earlier that evening and took a taxicab home just after closing time. Police were unable to locate the cab driver that he had that night.

In October 1975, police offered $2000 a reward for any information leading to the arrest and conviction of the murderer. The house owner also had some of his credit cards stolen that night. One of the credit cards was used in three stores and a motel in Moncton, New Brunswick, by a man in his early twenties with an average build. Detective Donald Sangster was sent to Moncton to collect any evidence or witness statements. Sangster was unable to find anything significant. The only thing police could find out about Walkley was that he was a communist activist who gave rally speeches in public places, which could have made him a target as well. This case remains unsolved.

2. **Fred John Fontaine,** a CBC employee, was 32 years old when he was found on **December 20, 1975**, badly beaten and bleeding in the bathroom of a gay tavern, the St. Charles Tavern. Police could not find any significant clues at the bar as many people had been there that evening, and when they saw the body, dozens of people went in and out of the bathroom. He was still alive and rushed to the hospital, where he remained in a coma and would eventually die about seven months later. This case remains unsolved.

3. **James Taylor Douglas** was a 41-year-old house painter who lived at 147 Elmhurst Avenue in Toronto. Police received a call where his body was found badly beaten to death with a baseball bat on **February 11, 1976**. The bat had belonged to Douglas, so the killer must have seen it in his house on the night of the murder. The only clue of significance that police got while canvassing the neighbors was that a pick-up truck was seen outside his home.

4. On the morning of **September 20, 1976**, the body of 59-year-old **James Stewart Kennedy** was found naked, beaten, and strangled to death in his home located at 262 Jarvis street. The murder weapon was a hand towel which came from Kennedy's house. Kennedy was an employee of the Department of National Revenue and was last seen at the St. Charles Tavern the previous Saturday evening. Police were unable to find a motive, and this case remains unsolved.

5. On **January 23, 1977,** the 25-year-old financial planner **Brian Latocki** left his job at the Toronto Dominion Bank early that day as he wasn't feeling very well. Later that night, he was seen at the St. Charles Tavern, a famous gay club at the time. The following Tuesday, after Latocki didn't show up for work, his supervisor  called his apartment and got no answer. Knowing Latocki reasonably well, he knew this wasn't normal, so he called the landlord of the apartment building at 141 Erskine Avenue. The landlord couldn't get an answer to his door, so he called the police. When the police arrived, he opened the door, and they entered the apartment. Latocki had been stripped naked and tied to his bed. It looked like he had been beaten badly on his face and head while still alive, probably to make him suffer. He was then strangled and stabbed. Latocki's apartment was locked, which was a clue as a person needed the key to lock or unlock the door unless you were inside the apartment. The beating was so bad that blood spattered all over the floor and walls. Medical examiners placed the time of death about 72 hours before his body was found. That would

mean he was probably killed late Friday night or early Saturday morning when he was last seen alive leaving the club. The apartment looked like it had been searched, perhaps for robbery purposes. This led to police using robbery as the motive for his murder. When Latocki was seen leaving the tavern on Friday night, he was with a man that looked to be in his mid-twenties, probably of East Indian descent. A reward of $10,000 was offered for information on the case, as with many Toronto murders and missing men. Latocki was keeping it secret that he was gay. Only for him, it was about not upsetting his traditional Ukraine family and keeping his job. The modern cases were usually men leading a straight-looking life and had a wife and children. His family learned of his homosexuality by reading it in the newspapers and television newscasts; very unsettling this would be for any family and friends. Over the forty-plus years, they had to live with what kind of a death he had and for what reason? Or who would do this to him? It creates a feeling of helplessness that you can't fix. You can't bring him back.

6. About 11 a.m. on **July 28, 1977**, police got a 911 call that a dead man was at an apartment on George Street in downtown Toronto. When police

arrived, they found 23-year-old Randall **Frederick Chidwick** stabbed to death in his apartment.

7. 62-YEAR-OLD **BERNARD GUAY** was walking in Allan Gardens Park on Horticultural Avenue on **May 5, 1977**, when he was attacked and beaten up. He was discovered in the park at about 12:15 a.m., still alive, and was rushed to the hospital. Guay died a few days later, on May 11th, from major blunt force  trauma to his head. Guay was from Quebec but had moved to Toronto over 25 years previously and worked in different restaurants until he became too blind to do the job correctly. He was living with 32-year-old Henri Carboit, who he had met on one of his previous restaurant jobs. They didn't have a sexual relationship and were just roommates. Police suggested that he was probably beaten up for making a sexual pass at someone else who was in the park who wasn't gay, as he was in the area of the park that was popular for gay cruising, or perhaps he was mugged. This case remains unsolved.

8. 35-YEAR-OLD **NEIL ROBERT WILKINSON** was found nude, beaten, and stabbed in his Charles Street East apartment on **December 15, 1977**. He had died from asphyxiation from his blood. Wilkinson was reported missing after he didn't show up for four shifts at his work, the Royal Bank. After canvassing the last place, he was  seen at the Parkside Tavern downtown, and they found out he was last seen around 1 a.m. at the club with two of his friends.

In January, a homeless man named James Allan Walker was arrested while drinking in the Parkside Tavern and charged with the first-degree murder of Wilkinson. Walker would arrange a plea of manslaughter with the crown prosecutor, but the judge overhearing the case rejected that plea and made him stand trial.

In court, Walker told the jury that he was with Wilkinson, and they were talking about life, and out of nowhere, Wilkinson brought up sexual fantasies. Walker claimed they weren't at Wilkinson's apartment to have sex, only to talk. During this conversation, Wilkinson began telling him about the different times he had sex with young boys, which angered Walker to the point of rage where he ended up attacking and beating him to death. Things were missing in this story; when they were having this conversation, they were nude, and Wilkinson was tied up with ropes. Police later, after talking with several of Wilkinson's friends, found out that he was into bondage-type sex. This is probably why he was tied up, and the two were having or about to have sex. Walker had then stomped on Wilkinson while he was tied up and helpless. He stomped on his face so hard that he hurt his feet. After killing Wilkinson, he showered and ate some of Wilkinson's food out of his fridge before getting dressed and leaving the apartment.

Walker would be convicted of second-degree murder and sentenced to twelve years in prison. One of the most interesting things about this case was that shortly before Walker was arrested, Chief Inspector George Sellars said at a press conference that he suspected the same man probably committed the murders of Wilkinson, James Kennedy, and Arthur Harold Walkley. This started the talk amongst the gay community in Toronto. Walker would be released from prison in 1990, and by 1996, he was back in for trafficking drug charges.

9. **Donald Rochester** was 47 years old and worked as a bartender and part-time handyman at Club 44, a lawn tennis club. On **February 13, 1978**, he was found dead at the club when other employees came to work their shifts. Rochester had been shot in the head.

When police arrived, they initially believed it was some robbery that went bad because he was missing a wallet. Later that day, police discovered that Rochester's wallet had been locked in the trunk of his car and not stolen. A strange thing about the crime scene was Rochester was wearing only a t-shirt and nothing else. Detectives assumed that he was probably forced to undress by the thief so that he wouldn't chase him after he left.

Almost two years later, a 19-year-old man named Fred Savage told one of his teachers that he had killed a man, but it was in self-defense. The teacher referred him to a lawyer she knew who took Savage into the police station on November 21, 1980, so he could tell detectives his story. At the time of the murder, Savage was sixteen years old, and he told police that Rochester was sexually assaulting him at the time, so he killed him to make it stop. Detectives noticed that Savage was a bit slower than an average man of 19 years, so they charged him with manslaughter.

At the trial, he claimed that Rochester pulled a gun out and forced him to perform sexual acts on him. During one of those sexual acts, he saw Rochester put the gun down, so he quickly grabbed the gun and shot at Rochester, only he missed. Rochester then jumped on Savage, and the two struggled over the weapon until Savage got control and shot him in the head. He might not have been charged if that was where he left it. Instead, he stood over Rochester and shot him point-blank twice.

Savage was convicted of manslaughter, sentenced to two years in a reformatory, and given three years probation. He was also forced to take psychiatric treatment and prohibited from possessing firearms for life.

10. **Shirley Hauser** was born Peter Christopher. She was a 20-year-old who lived as a trans woman. She was stabbed to death on **August 19, 1978,** on the school grounds of Western Technical College, located at Commercial High School on 125 Evelyn Crescent. Hauser had been living and dressing as a woman for several years and was now on hormone medication and having a sex change operation. Earlier in the day, Hauser

had met a man while she was swimming at the Sunnyside Public Recreational Center. Afterward, at around 4 a.m., the two of them went to the school. When they found her body, they spotted a trail of blood trailing away from the body for quite a distance, which they thought perhaps belonged to the assailant, which proved to be accurate as the blood didn't belong to Hauser.

Also of note, in Hauser's purse, she had hormone pills that were not hers and were much stronger than the pills prescribed for her. Police then checked out her apartment on Westminster Avenue, finding nothing significant. Later, police received a tip to go to an apartment about three kilometers from the crime scene. Detectives found a blood-spattered motorcycle and helmet in the parking garage, so they approached the landlady to find out which apartment the bike belonged to. The landlady told them and explained that she had been cleaning up blood drops from the apartment building entryway stairs all morning. When detectives went to the apartment, they met the renter, 20-year-old William Richard Andes, who told them he was visiting a friend who had been wounded. That's why there was blood on him and his bike.

After a few days more investigation and blood tests, police arrested Andes and charged him with second-degree murder. At the trial, Andes claimed that he flew into an uncontrollable rage after finding out that Hauser was a transexual and stabbed her seventeen times. He explained further that he would have killed her, which was self-defense. When he attacked her initially with the knife, she was able to get it away from the Andes, and a struggle ensued. During that struggle, he said that she stabbed and was trying to kill him, so when he got control of the knife, he just reacted and stabbed her until she stopped moving.

Andes was found guilty on April 9, 1979. During his sentencing in court, his mother was removed from the courthouse as she was screaming out loud, "Please don't punish him for the homosexual. Please, he is the victim." He only spent three years in prison before getting out. In April 1984, while he was still on parole, he was arrested for assaulting two sisters because they refused to have sex with him. For this crime, he would get another eight years in prison.

11. On **August 27, 1978**, 41-year-old **Colin Nicholson** and 56-year-old Albert Homer Durnan were at the horse stables on Church Street. During their time there, they met two men and spent the day together riding horses and talking. When they were done, Nicholson and Durnan invited the two men over to their

apartment on Joseph Street. Later that evening, a third man, a friend of the men they invited over for drinks, joined them at the apartment. Around 1:30 a.m., the three visiting men suddenly attacked both Nicholson and Durnan using whatever they could find out of the kitchen as a weapon, even a heavy iron skillet. Both men were knocked out, and during that time, the three visitors robbed them of cash, clothing, silverware, and liquor. Durnan was the first to come to and called the police and ambulance immediately. Nicholson eventually came around but was severely injured. The two men were taken to the hospital, where Durnan was treated and released, but Nicholson would succumb to his injuries. Later, the three men Brain Robert Pasher, Kerry Pierce Gallant, and John Stephen Sharkey Jr., were caught by police. They were all charged with assault and robbery, and Sharkey Jr. was also charged with manslaughter and would get an additional seven-year sentence.

12. 39-YEAR-OLD **GERALD DOUGLAS WHITE** was taking care of his friend's house by watering the lawn and plants and feeding the birds while they were on vacation. On **September 18, 1978**, White invited 23-year-old Paris Colin Rogers to accompany him while he took care of his friend's

place. After they watered the plants, they went inside to have a drink. An argument ensued. During that argument, Rogers hit White over his head, hard enough to kill him. Neighbors called the police, and Rogers, scared, took White's car and left the scene. Police caught him a short while later and recovered White's car. They arrested Rogers and charged him with second-degree murder.

At trial, Rogers claimed that he killed White only because he came on to him sexually and wouldn't take no for an answer. He was forced to hit him to make him stop. On April 30, 1979, Rogers was convicted of manslaughter and sentenced to six years in prison. The court believed that he killed White only in response to his sexual advances. But Rogers had a history of violence, including having killed before. In 1975, when Rogers was at a stag party, he beat another man to death in front of the whole group of men there. In that crime, again, he was convicted of manslaughter and only received two and a half years. On January 8, 1988, after Rogers got out of prison for killing White, he was again arrested for assaulting a man. This time it was Rogers trying to force a man to perform sexual acts on him because he wouldn't. Rogers beat him with a steel pipe. In that case, he was charged with robbery, aggravated assault, and forcible confinement.

While waiting for sentencing on this case, he was arrested another time for carrying a gun unlawfully and being in a fight at a donut shop. But before he would go to court for that charge or be sentenced for the previous charge, he was stabbed to death just outside a strip club in Toronto.

13. On **September 20, 1978**, the manager of the Studio II discotheque, 29-year-old **Alexander Sandy LeBlanc**,  was found bleeding to death in his apartment at 16 St. Joseph Court. He would die shortly after he was found. He was the second gay man to be murdered in just two days, shocking the Toronto gay community. He had been a manager and co-owner of two popular gay bars in town—one of them was Club David, which mysteriously burned down on New Year's Day that same year. This case was highly violent and looked like a significant struggle and fight. LaBlanc was stabbed like all previous victims were, too, only it was a much more brutal attack as he had been stabbed well over 100 times throughout his body, including his head, face, stomach, legs, and feet. After several days of nobody hearing from him, some friends kicked in his apartment door to find his

dead body lying on the floor. When police arrived, they discovered several footprint impressions on the blood-soaked carpet in his apartment, which seemed to go to his window. They found semen and blood everywhere, from his bed to the window. Only back in the seventies, there was no DNA testing available. This case remains unsolved.

14. Another gay man, 25-year-old **William Duncan Robinson**, was found stabbed to death in his Vaughn Street apartment on **November 28, 1978**. When he was discovered,  police said he had already been dead for two days. Police checked on Robinson only after his sister reported that he had not shown up for work at the Royal Bank for two shifts in a row, and she couldn't get any answer from him on the phone. Like some of the other crime scenes police had been to in the last few years, it looked like the assailant had been injured and the victim. When detectives canvassed his neighbors, quite a few said they either heard loud music playing or some strange hollow-sounding noises coming from his apartment a couple of nights beforehand. Robinson was last seen at the St. Charles Tavern

at around 2 a.m. two nights prior, and he was with another man. Police released a composite sketch and description of that man. The man was in his late twenties, 6 foot 5 inches tall, had long greasy brown hair, dirty hands, foul-smelling body odor, and a scruffy goatee. He had also been trying to buy some drugs while at the tavern. Police offered a $10,000 reward for any evidence leading to the arrest and prosecution of the murderer. This case remains unsolved.

19

MURDER OF EMANUEL JAQUES

One murder in the later 1970s that sparked things to come only isolated the gay community more from the police. It happened on July 28, 1977, when a 12-year-old boy, Emanuel Jaques, was offered $35 to help move some equipment to a local downtown Toronto business. Jaques had worked as a shoeshine boy on the main gay strip on Yonge Street, so he was familiar with the businesses and many people working there. So, when the Charlie's Angels Massage Parlor asked him to help them move some photography equipment from their office for $35, he jumped at the chance to make some quick money.

Three doormen let him in when he arrived at the store: Robert Wayne Kribs, Joseph Woods, and Werner Gruener. Once inside the parlor, he met the guy who offered him the job, Saul David Betesh, a sex worker. The four men lured Jaques into the office, tied him up, and took turns sexually assaulting him for about twelve hours before strangling him and finally drowning him in a bathroom sink. The men then hid the body in a wood pile on the roof of the business's building.

A few days later, Betesh told a well-known gay activist in the community, George Hislop, about the rape and murder of the boy. Hislop connected Betesh with his personal lawyer, who arranged to have him surrender to the police. During his interrogation, Betesh told detectives about what he and the other three men did to the boy and told them where they could find those men. The three men were arrested later that day, and all four were charged with the rape and murder of Jaques. Kribs pleaded guilty to first-degree murder, and Betesh was tried for the same charge and was found guilty of first-degree murder. Woods would be convicted of second-degree murder while Gruener was acquitted as police could only prove that he let Jaques into the building.

Jaques's murder and sexual assault caused massive outrage in not only Toronto but all of Canada. Protests broke out every day for weeks to demand that the city clean up the Yonge Street area where they wanted all gay bookstores, massage parlors, and bathhouses closed. Several of these protests also asked for capital punishment to be brought back.

The tension between the gay community and the police department in Toronto continued into the early eighties with the bathhouse raids in 1981. Over 250 men were arrested out of four bathhouses in a one-night raid. They entered by breaking through doors, and when inside, they destroyed much of the property, including the men's lockers.

Even though there were numerous murders of men in the gay community, they were somehow overshadowed by the murder of Jaques. The details of these murders didn't matter. Today, it's easy to look back and realize the obvious similarities between these cases: all fourteen men were homosexual, most were found naked in their apartments, stabbed, strangled, beaten, and their apartments were robbed. Quite a few of them were last seen leaving the St. Charles Tavern and were members of the gay community.

The City of Toronto and the entire country had their minds on returning to the death penalty and cleaning up these gay communities from their sexually promiscuous ways. The tension would result in the gay murders disappearing from the media and public's minds and soon after being forgotten.

With all the commonalities and all the murders occurring within three and a half years, police still wouldn't say they were connected, and there was no serial killer. Whether this was because police truly believed it or wanted to tell the public this so as not to scare them is still in debate.

In the seventies, police wanted nothing to do with the gay community, and the feeling was mutual. So, with that kind of relationship, there was no effort to try and solve these crimes together by both groups pooling their resources and working together. I am not sure whether the relationship was that of opponents or not. They simply didn't know each other very well, and the gay community was ignored.

20

MORE MURDERS IN GAY VILLAGE 2017

Also missing and murdered during this time in Toronto's Gay Village were a transgender woman named Alloura Wells and a woman named Tess Richey. At the time, with the disappearances of Selim Esen, Andrew Kinsman, Alloura Wells, and Tess Richey, the community feared a serial killer was at large. However, the police insisted the cases were not linked.

ALLOURA WELLS NOVEMBER 2017

Alloura Wells was one of four children born to Mike and Mary Wells in 1990, who lived in Toronto, where her mother was a

Tim Horton's manager, and her father worked odd labor and construction jobs around the area. As a teenager, Wells would sneak out of home and go to the Gay Village part of Toronto, where she could watch all the drag shows. She soon became friends with a lot of the performers.

When Wells turned eighteen, she told her family that she was transgender and wanted to live as a woman. The family was okay with the news and was supportive throughout her transition. When she turned 22 years old in 2012, Wells rented an apartment in the suburb of Scarborough to be close to her sister. Her mother died in February 2013, and soon after, her father and brother became homeless as her mother financially supported the household. After her mother died, the family unity disappeared.

Wells was eventually evicted from her apartment for nonpayment of her rent, so she bought a tent, pitched it in the Rosedale Ravine Lands Park, and made that her home. She had fallen on hard times, traveled around with her tent, and stayed wherever she could.

She committed small thefts to get food and other items but was eventually caught and ended up with a short sentence in the Vanier Centre for Women. Wells also occasionally turned to survival sex work for money.

Her only known romantic relationship was

with Augustinus Balesdent, and he was an intravenous drug user himself and couldn't help her financially or with a place to live. Her father got an apartment in March 2017 and offered for her to stay there with him, but she refused. This was the last time that he saw her alive. Wells's last Facebook post was on July 26, 2017.

On August 5, 2017, when Rebecca Price and one of her best friends were hiking in the Rosedale Ravine Park in the midtown area of Toronto, they came across what looked like a dead woman. The police were called and roped off the scene after arriving. The body was discovered outside a tent with what looked like a syringe beside her. The woman was well dressed in women's clothing and make-up, not messy. They could not find any identification on her or in the tent, so they listed her as a Jane Doe. In the dead woman's purse, police found what appeared to be a blonde wig.

The body was taken to the medical examiner, and a complete autopsy was conducted. The body was so badly decomposed that they could not find the cause of death. The woman was probably dead for at least three weeks, and they couldn't identify her. They were able to determine that she was a transgender female.

Strangely enough, the Toronto Police department decided not to make a press release or any statement about finding the dead body, which was against their standard procedure. They later said this was because they had no details to release and wanted to work more on the case first to gather some information to give to the media.

In early November, her father searched through the drug rehab centers and jails around the Toronto area for his daughter. He discovered that his daughter had not been in any of them recently, and he filed a missing person report with the police. The police immediately looked for her on-again, off-again boyfriend, Augustus, but couldn't find him anywhere.

After police realized there was a possibility that the body found might be Alloura Wells, they went to her family and got a DNA sample to do a comparison test. On November 23, 2017, the Ontario Centre of Forensic Services confirmed that the body found was Alloura Wells. Her murder is still unsolved.

TESS RICHEY NOVEMBER 2017

The youngest of five daughters, Tess Richey, was born on November 30 of 1994. She was a marathon runner, completed her flight service program, and applied to the major airlines for a job. While waiting to hear back from the airlines, she worked odd jobs around downtown Toronto.

It was Friday, November 24, 2017. Tess spent almost the whole day with her sister Rachel at her Toronto home, playing video games and eating. At 11:30 that evening, she left to meet her friend at the Church Street clubs that attracted many young people.

Richey and her friend drank a lot of alcohol until about 1:30 in the morning, when they left the last bar they were in. While walking down the main street, they stopped and talked with a couple who lived there. Soon after, Richey's friend got a text from her boyfriend, who was waiting at home for her, so she took the streetcar home. It was about 4 a.m.

The following day Rachel texted her sister at 8:45 the morning but got no answer. Later that night, she looked at the message she had sent to her sister and realized that the message was never delivered. She began to get worried and decided to check with the hospitals, and with no luck, she finally called the police to report her missing.

Tess's mother remembered that she had let her daughter use her Fitbit account, so they checked on Tess's activity that night. The account showed that Tess had taken 300 steps just after 3 am that night. The next action was at 4 am when Tess booked a ride from Uber, but it was later cancelled before it got to the location to pick her up.

The police search for Tess was conducted by the division closest to where she lived and not where she was last seen alive. On November 20, 2017, Tess's family and friends went to the Church Street neighborhood, put posters of Tess up, and went door to door asking if anyone had seen her.

Two days into the search, Tess's body was found by her family members very near where she was last seen at the bottom of a narrow stairway which led to a basement suite. When police got to the body and looked over the crime scene, they decided that the death was not suspicious but still sent the body to have an autopsy. The medical examiner's report said that Tess died from neck compression, and her death was ruled a homicide.

The homicide detectives in Toronto got the case on December 1, where they canvassed the neighborhood and checked for any video cameras in the area to see if they could spot anything suspicious. In the video, they recovered police found a man that Tess was last seen with that evening and had a press conference with his picture and information to try and find him.

It appears that Tess and her girlfriend went to a food cart and got hot dogs, and while they were there, she met the man they were now looking for and trying to identify. The video then showed Tess and the unknown man walking away together and going down an alley off of Church Street. The last time she is seen on video is again with her and the strange man going down the stairwell where her body would later be found.

The suspect was later identified and located at his apartment, where he was arrested on February 4, 2018. The next day his name was released as 21-year-old Kalen Schlatter, and he was charged with second-degree murder. Schlatter was not granted parole and remained in custody which was unusual as he had no previous criminal record. The police wouldn't give the reason to the press, saying there was a publication ban on the case.

When he appeared in court on December 31, Schlatter's charges were upped to first-degree murder, and his trial would begin on January 13, 2020. And after about six weeks of testimony and evidence being presented, he was found guilty.

21

POLICE REVIEW

The Toronto Police Department was greatly criticized for failing to find Tess Richey's body two doors next to where she was last seen. Instead, her remains were found by her mother and friends, who were out walking the streets and actively searching. The family found her easily two days after the police started their investigation. Several news reports were made at the time in Canada where the Toronto Police Department spokesperson said there were concerns about the professionalism in the beginning stages of the investigation on this missing person case.

    The talk around the community was that the Toronto Police always prioritize their missing person cases based on the person who is missing and the circumstances surrounding them going missing. In Tess' particular case, the detectives didn't call uniformed police to help in their search unless they believed there was an actual kidnapping or murder.

In the Summer of 2018, two Toronto officers were charged with misconduct and neglect of duty. They were also charged and found guilty of not reporting the case to their superior officer. It turns out that both officers had responded to the missing person's call and were told about where the victim was last seen. But they never even went to the location to conduct a basic search. Richey's body was found only 130 feet from where those officers responded.

Toronto Police Chief Mark Saunders held a press conference on December 8, 2017, responding to the two deaths (Alloura Wells and Tess Richey) and two missing men from the Church and Wellesley Streets (Selim Esen and Andrew Kinsman). The gay community thought for sure that there was a serial killer who was targetting gay men and their friends. Still, Saunders tried to reassure them that there was no evidence of a serial killer or that any of the crimes were connected.

It is important to mention that the Toronto police get over 4000 reports of missing people every year, but most of them are resolved relatively quickly and usually without any police investigation. During the time that McArthur was active, from about 2014 to 2018, 600 missing person reports were made to the police. Around thirty cases remain unsolved and open.

One problem is that whenever men go missing, it doesn't create as much panic as when women or children go missing. There is a belief that men can and will take care of themselves—not only in law enforcement's eyes but also in the general public. Generally, it is assumed that men are stronger and less likely to be kidnapped or taken for some nefarious reason, such as human trafficking or something else.

But because so many missing persons are reported in Toronto, police must first consider the circumstances surrounding the missing person. They need to find as much information as possible about the missing person, such as character or behaviors. If the person is a harmful drug addict or alcoholic who constantly floats around the city with no home, they are likely just passed out somewhere and will turn up soon. That's the general thought in police circles.

There are about eleven missing reports every day in Toronto. With only so many resources available to police, they have to quickly examine each case and decide where best to put their workforce to help find the person. If a fifteen-year-old girl was out shopping with her mother in a grocery store and a known drug addict on the street disappeared, they have to assess that quickly and send two men to find the girl.

I am sure that most of the police force in Toronto want to be able to find any missing person, no matter who they are or how they live. Still, there will always be a few officers who will judge people because of their lifestyle or circumstances. The lack of activity or investigation always leads to accusations that the police do not care about minority groups, homeless people, and drug addicts.

We must remember that we deal with human beings on both sides, including the missing person and law enforcement. All humans have emotions and feelings that always lead to both excellent and destructive behaviors.

Another problem is that humans make mistakes. The police officer can be someone who has not been trained very well or perhaps has had no training in missing person cases. There is a lack of confidence and sometimes even fear regarding the police. In the last few years, we have seen more police held accountable for misconduct and more focus on training officers in mental health.

The lack of training or inadequately trained officers leads us to incompetence in an investigation. The officer might not do a thorough check on a victim or suspect. They might miss evidence left in the open for anybody to find.

These topics are not meant to criticize or blame officers out on the job trying to do the best for their community. There is no blame here. It's just the facts of what we, as a society, have to deal with and its results. The intent is so that we can fix these things.

Mentioning these topics is also not to blame anybody who has been a victim or gone missing for any reason. Harmful lifestyle or drugs and alcohol addiction are real issues in our society; we all need to discuss these problems to find an answer.

Looking back through the 2014 to 2017 years in Toronto and how these cases were handled, everyone can agree that things should have been done better. We must go through the steps taken throughout the missing persons and murders and find a resolution to how we want these cases handled by law enforcement in the future.

A significant finding of the internal police investigation that followed this case was that in handling these investigations, detectives didn't make any connections between the missing and murdered victims reported to them. Some of the public believed that because the victims were gay, immigrants, or drug users, the police didn't care about them. Others in the general public thought that police were incompetent, overwhelmed, and didn't have enough manpower to investigate these cases properly.

On February 29, 2018, the police released some of their internal investigation findings, which showed several officers working under tremendous stress, anxiety, and burnout. It showed how short of staff the police department was and that the Toronto Police Department had been reduced by five hundred officers from 2010 to 2017 alone.

The police internal probe on the Richey missing person case determined that the responding officer had procedural and training gaps. In particular when receiving and understanding the information given when a crime is reported.

In Alloura Wells' case, her family told the investigation that those police officers said to them that their case was not a high priority because Alloura had been homeless for several years. This opinion was supported because when she was reported missing, it was November, and her body wasn't discovered until the following year, in August. Her body had been decomposed to the point that it took them another three months to identify her.

The 2017 Pride Parade even banned the Toronto Police Department from attending because of its poor investigation and lack of caring in the missing person cases of gay people from the community.

On February 20, 2018, the Ontario Court of Justice ordered the release of documents used by the Toronto police during their investigation of Bruce McArthur. Within this 220-page document, there were some critical oversights during the investigation. One of the detectives recognized McArthur from the 2012 Project Houston investigation about the *Zambian Meat* website and the missing gay men from Toronto. Still, Detective Joshua McKenzie didn't remember that he had interviewed McArthur for those cases until September of 2017, after police realized that Bruce McArthur's van was seen picking up Andrew Kinsmen from his apartment the day he went missing. As well, just eighteen days after he interviewed McArthur for Project Houston, McArthur bought a new vehicle, a 2001 silver Dodge Caravan. Years later, McArthur purchased another new vehicle two weeks after the disappearance of Andrew Kinsman.

On Tuesday, April 13, 2021, Ontario Judge Gloria Epstein released the findings of her two-year review of the Toronto police's handling of missing person cases in the city over the Bruce McArthur years. Epstein's report exposed a series of failures by the police department regarding their procedures in investigating the missing men and McArthur.

22

SURVIVORS

SEAN CRIBBIN

In March 2018, Sean Cribbin told *Global News* in Canada that he had met McArthur and knew who he was. The two had met on different gay dating apps and talked quite a bit. Finally, in the Summer of 2017, they set up a time and place to meet. McArthur picked up Cribbin to take him back to his apartment. During the ride there, they discussed the ground rules for what their sexual encounter was going to be. Cribbin had mentioned the serial killer of the Toronto gay village, but he got no response from McArthur.

Cribbin wanted McArthur to make a cocktail using GHB and gave him the instructions on the correct amount to use so that he wouldn't become incapacitated. McArthur had told Cribbin how much experience he had with making GHB cocktails and BDSM. When the two began, Cribbin started to have problems breathing; he started sweating a lot, which was unusual for him. The next thing he knew, he blacked out.

When Cribbin began to come around, he heard noises coming from the apartment's other bedroom. As soon as he could, he got up and told McArthur that he was leaving because his roommate had come home. He didn't even wait for McArthur to offer him a ride home. He just left.

About six months later, McArthur was arrested. When Cribbin heard the news, and once he saw his face on the television, he remembered the last time they had seen each other and began to think about what would have happened to him if McArthur's roommate hadn't come home that day.

About one week after McArthur's arrest, police contacted Cribbin and asked him to come for an interview. After he arrived, police started asking him about his encounter with McArthur on that day he was taken to his apartment. Halfway through his explanation to the police, an officer asked him if he had seen any cameras at McArthur's apartment that day. Cribbin couldn't remember anything but was shocked when they showed him pictures taken while he was passed out and naked on McArthur's bed. A few photographs even had Cribbin handcuffed and McArthur using a metal bar to make it look like he was choking him while they were on his bed.

MATT MACKINNON

MacKinnon worked with McArthur at the Garden Center in Milton, Ontario, in 2011 when McArthur sub-contracted him to build three water features for one of his customers in his landscaping business.

"Well, he had a project going, and I bid on the job. He really liked that he could pick out his own materials.

McArthur was a very personable person with a great sense of humor. He was very conscientious about his landscaping customers being happy. He was the easiest guy to work with and always paid me on time.

I think he had somewhere around ten different properties that he was taking care of regularly. He not only kept them cleaned up and looking good, but he would design tropical planters for them.

His customers loved him because of his hard work and creativity.

If I remember correctly, for about the first five years, he had a business partner who worked with him who would come to the properties about two or three times a year. McArthur also had several younger laborers who came and did work at the different jobs, but that always changed. They were never around long enough to get to know any of them. The laborers were always average age of about thirty or forty years old, and quite often, they were brown-skinned. In fact, most of them didn't seem to understand or speak English.

One man who worked for McArthur that I d0 remember was Andrew Kinsman. He was really easy to remember because he didn't look like most of the others. He was white, a big man with a distinctive mustache and beard. He looked like a man who could work hard and be a good laborer, whereas most of the men McArthur brought to the landscaping jobs had just an average build and didn't really seem cut out for that kind of work. I also didn't get the impression that they were in any kind of relationship. It looked pretty professional. Like boss and employee.

Most of his customers really seemed to like Bruce as he would always hang around with them and talk to them for a while after the job was done, even have a glass of wine or something. His customers were usually over 60 years old and quite well off.

I was really shocked to hear about Bruce being arrested for murder. My ex-wife was the first person to tell me, and she was shocked too. It's still really hard to believe as Bruce wasn't conceded or aggressive at all and was always very friendly. He never struck me as that kind of guy, either by his demeanor or physically by his size. I feel really sorry for any of his customers who had to come home to find out the sort of things that he was burying on their properties."

ISSAAC

"I was on *Silver Daddies* sometime back in 2011, and he had struck up a chat with me. I had been with other guys a few

> times by then, and he was nice, saying that he liked my profile. I was living in Toronto at the time and never really went out to clubs or bars much as it wasn't my thing. I mainly just worked and would come home, eat, and watch some TV. He seemed really nice and not aggressive at all, and we decided to meet."

For the next few years, the two men would become intimate and get together just for a sexual encounter every once in a while.

> "He was always gentle, and after we had sex, he would tell me about his life. Something like the divorce he was going through with his wife or about his two kids. Bruce told me that he was outed to his family and that he never had a chance to tell them himself. He also figured this was the reason that they were getting the divorce. If he would have been able to tell her himself, they would probably still be living together today.
> Even though we talked about some of our personal stuff, I never thought of him as a boyfriend or possible long-term

partner. It was just a casual thing, maybe a friend-with-benefits type thing. We always would meet at my place, never his. He would always text me first before coming over if he wanted to hook up, but if he was just looking to visit me or something like that, he could just show up without notice.

Bruce said he wanted to keep it secret about him being gay and about the two of them hooking up for sex. I guess in some ways, he was still in the closet. One thing that he also did often was come to my apartment building and wait in the parking lot for me to get home from work. Before I would get my car parked, all of a sudden, he would appear in front of me.

On June 20, 2016, I just got home from work, and he was in my apartment building parking lot, just as he had done before. I told him to come on up, and I would have to shower first as I got really dirty at work today. Bruce told me that he didn't want to go up to his apartment this time. Instead, he wanted to have sex in the van, as it would be far more exciting."

So, the two men agreed to meet at a shopping

plaza not too far away from Issac's apartment after he had a chance to clean up first. It was around 6:30 when Issac finally got to the plaza parking lot, and he pulled up beside McArthur, who was standing outside beside his van. As soon as Issac got out of his vehicle, McArthur, in a quick panicked voice, told him to get in his van and get down, so he did.

The back of the van had been cleared of its seats, so there was enough room to lay down. Some tarps and a fur coat were lying on the van floor for him to lay on instead of the bare metal floor.

Issac lay and waited for McArthur to get in the van, and after he did, he took off his clothes and laid on top of Issac with his full body weight. McArthur then grabbed Issac's arm with one hand and grabbed his throat with the other. He began to squeeze tightly around Issac's neck. Issac began to fight back hard and soon gained his escape, where he then called 911 to report what had happened.

23

TODD MCARTHUR

Todd McArthur was Bruce McArthur's youngest child, born in 1981. Throughout his teens and adulthood, he has had several legal issues that Bruce had always tried to handle. But with so many of his own problems, there wasn't much time for Todd's.

Starting around the age of eleven or so in 1993, Todd began to make phone calls to other girls. But these weren't your regular phone calls. Todd would call the girls names or say something sexual to them. When his parents found out, he received a stern talking to and was grounded. His bad behavior happened at school as well as at his home. At school, he would call the girls walking by him in the halls bad names. When any of the girls confronted him, he only became more berating.

The school gave Todd detentions or sent him home for the day, with a threat of being suspended for longer.

Over the next twenty years, this behavior continued, and he received more than two dozen convictions for making these harassing phone calls.

In 2014, 33-year-old Todd saw a woman's picture on a website, and for some reason, he became obsessed with her. He studied the website to find as much information as possible about her, including where she lived and her phone number. The two had never met before and had no history, including with their friends and family. For over two months, he called her and repeatedly made sexual remarks in a very aggressive tone. He also called her, whispered her name, and then hung up. These calls scared the victim even more as she had no idea who it was or what provoked such behavior toward her.

Todd was making these calls from his home in Oshawa, Ontario. His victim lived in Kitchener, Ontario, about 165 kilometers away or about two hours of driving time from each other. Not only was he calling her phone, but he went to a website called *myex.com*, where you could post pictures and comments about an ex of yours who did something wrong while you were together with them. This site was meant to be a place where you could warn others before they found more victims. Todd took a picture of the woman he was calling, altered the photo to make it look like she was naked, and put it up on this website.

The calls were eventually traced to Todd McArthur's residence, and when police did a background check on the family, they discovered 24 convictions of Todd for making harassing phone calls. Todd was arrested and brought in for evaluation and questioning.

During his psychological reviews, he was diagnosed with a disorder called "Telephone Scatalogia." He had been previously diagnosed with this problem and received some treatments. This disorder is usually tied to depression around a person's first sexual experience. Todd's case probably had something to do with the harassing phone calls he made when he was eleven or twelve.

Todd received a 24-month jail term, on top of the three months he had already served in jail during the trial, plus a recommendation for intensive counseling at a clinic in Brampton, Ontario. The judge at his trial told McArthur to take his treatment seriously as he needed to curb his bad behavior and that if he ever got into this kind of trouble again, he would end up in the penitentiary. He was also placed on three years of probation after being released from jail and could only be released to a stable home.

When he got out of jail, he went to live with his father, who already had a previous conviction of assault and was on probation himself. The judge didn't know about his father's latest legal problems.

When he arrived at his father's place, Bruce put him to work at his landscaping business to try and keep him busy and out of trouble. But instead of staying out of trouble, in November 2015, he started doing it again. This time, his three months of harassing phone calls were to a woman who lived in Oshawa. Todd was caught again and arrested. After serving a short sentence, he was released on probation and again allowed to move back into his father's apartment.

In early 2018, he committed another series of harassing phone calls and was charged. Todd, now 37 years old, appeared in the 150 Bond Street Courthouse in Oshawa on February 8, 2018, for breaching his probation after making more indecent phone calls.

TIMELINE OF EVENTS

September 2010 – 40-year-old Skandaraj "Skanda" Navaratnam disappeared from the Toronto Gay Village.

December 9, 2010 – Abdulbasir "Basir" Faizi, 42 years old, was reported missing from his wife to the Peel Regional Police Department when he didn't return home from his job.

October 2012 – 58-year-old Majeed Kayhan from Toronto is reported missing.

November 2012 – The Toronto Police Department launched Project Houston to investigate the three gay men who had gone missing from the Toronto Gay Village and the *Zambian Meat* cannibal website.

April 2014 – Police decide to shut down Project Houston without finding the victims or solving the cannibal connection to the missing men.

August 2015 – 50-year-old Soroush Mahmudi is reported missing from Toronto.

May 2016 – July 2017 – Dean Lisowick, 43 years old at the time. McArthur killed him.

April 14, 2017 – Selim Esen is reported missing, last seen walking on Bloor Street. He was

44 years old at the time.

June 26, 2017 – 49-year-old Andrew Kinsman goes missing and is last seen around Parliament Street.

August 2017 – Toronto Police Department initiate Project Prism to investigate the disappearances of both Esen and Kinsman.

September 2017 – Bruce McArthur becomes a suspect for detectives.

December 8, 2017 – Toronto Police Chief Mark Saunders holds a press conference declaring that there was no serial killer in Toronto.

❖

January 17, 2018 – Detectives discover

evidence that McArthur was responsible for the deaths of Kinsman and Esen.

❖

January 18, 2018 – McArthur is arrested and charged with first-degree murder for both Kinsman and Esen's murders.

❖

January 19, 2018 – Bruce McArthur appears in court.

❖

January 29, 2018 – McArthur gets an additional three first-degree murder charges for the deaths of Mahmudi, Kayhan, and Lisowick.

❖

February 8, 2018 – Police discovered Andrew Kinsman's remains.

❖

February 23, 2018 – Bruce McArthur gets an additional first-degree murder charge for the death of Skandaraj Navaratnam after his remains were discovered.

March 5, 2018 – Detectives hold a press conference displaying a photograph of a dead man they thought to have been a victim of McArthur with the hopes that the public could identify him. They also say that they discovered the remains of another man, the seventh now.

April 11, 2018 – Bruce McArthur is charged with his seventh first-degree murder for the death of Abdulbasir "Basir" Faizi.

April 16, 2018 – Bruce McArthur is charged again, now his eighth first-degree murder charge, this time for the death of Krishna Kumar Kanagaratnam.

January 29, 2019 – Bruce McArthur pleaded guilty to all eight murder charges.

❖

February 8, 2019 – Bruce McArthur is sentenced to life in prison without a chance for parole for a minimum of twenty-five years.

REFERENCES

1. Scoboni, Lee: "Tied and Tortured," *Murder Village: Stories of Murder in Toronto's Gay Village,* https://murdervillage.com/1977/01/25/tied-and-tortured/
2. Cowley, Sawyer: "Stomped to Death," *Murder Village: Stories of Murder in Toronto's Gay Village,* https://murdervillage.com/1977/12/15/stomped-to-death/
3. Scoboni, Lee: "Trouble on Borden," *Murder Village: Stories of Murder in Toronto's Gay Village,* https://murdervillage.com/1975/02/18/trouble-on-borden/
4. Scoboni, Lee: "Unsolved Baseball Bat Murder," *Murder Village: Stories of Murder in Toronto's Gay Village,* https://murdervillage.com/1976/02/11/unsolved-baseball-bat-murder/
5. Cowley, Sawyer: "Last Seen At St. Charles Tavern," *Murder Village: Stories of Murder in Toronto's Gay Village,* https://murdervillage.com/1976/09/20/last-seen-at-st-charles-tavern/
6. Scoboni, Lee: "Mugging Becomes Murder," *Murder Village: Stories of Murder in Toronto's Gay Village,* https://murdervillage.com/1977/05/05/mugging-becomes-murder/

7. Scoboni, Lee: "A Strange Hollow Sound," *Murder Village: Stories of Murder in Toronto's Gay Village*, https://murdervillage.com/1978/11/28/a-strange-hollow-sound/
8. Scoboni, Lee: "Victim Was An Assailant," *Murder Village: Stories of Murder in Toronto's Gay Village*, https://murdervillage.com/1978/02/13/victim-was-an-assailant/
9. Scoboni, Lee: "Swimming Leads to Murder," *Murder Village: Stories of Murder in Toronto's Gay Village*, https://murdervillage.com/1978/08/19/swimming-leads-to-murder/
10. Cowley, Sawyer: "Robbed and Beaten to Death," *Murder Village: Stories of Murder in Toronto's Gay Village*, https://murdervillage.com/1978/09/04/robbed-and-beaten-to-death/
11. Cowley, Sawyer: "Flowers and Feathers," *Murder Village: Stories of Murder in Toronto's Gay Village*, https://murdervillage.com/1978/09/17/flowers-and-feathers/
12. Cowley, Sawyer: "Nine Stab Wounds," *Murder Village: Stories of Murder in Toronto's Gay Village*, https://murdervillage.com/1979/03/18/nine-stab-wounds/
13. Isai, Vjosa: "Gay Village stalked by a serial killer . . . a second time?," *The Hamilton Spectator*, February 2, 2018, https://www.thespec.com/news/ontario/2018/02/02/gay-village-stalked-by-a-serial-killer-a-second-time.html

14. Alexander Wood at the *Dictionary of Canadian Biography*.
15. "Del Newbigging, 1934–2012" at the Wayback Machine. *Xtra Magazine*.
16. Winsa, Patty: "Before Pride, there was a kiss: Toronto gay activists look back on 1976 protest," *Toronto Star*, June 27, 2015.
17. Drag queens on Halloween, *CBC* Archives.
18. Tattelman, Ira: (2005-01-01). "Toronto Police Raid Gay Bathhouses." *GLBT History*, 1976-1987. EBSCO Publishing. pp. 127–130.
19. Gillis, Wendy: "Toronto police officer who released Bruce McArthur years before serial killer's final capture is cleared of misconduct," *Toronto Star*, August 23, 2021. https://www.thestar.com/news/gta/2021/08/23/toronto-cop-who-released-bruce-mcarthur-years-before-serial-killers-final-capture-is-cleared-of-misconduct.html
20. Gillis, Wendy: "A police officer with 'tunnel-vision' or a scapegoat for the botched Bruce McArthur investigation? Discipline case hears closing arguments," *Toronto Star*, May 21, 2021.
21. "Raids have gays steaming," *Vancouver Sun Newspaper*, Sunday, February 6, 1981.
22. "Not the Shadowy Night Town," *Macleans Canada* Article, January 12, 1981.

23. Farris: Nick: "A Monster that preyed on our city," *Vancouver Sun Newspaper*, Wednesday, January 30, 2019, Page NP2.
24. Farris, Nick: "Pure evil: McArthur receives a life sentence," *Vancouver Sun* Newspaper, Saturday February 9, 2019, Page NP2.
25. Gillis, Wendy: "Man who was Choked in Bruce McArthur's van, shares how he escaped," *Toronto Star*, Monday, March 25, 2019.
26. Powell, Batsey: "Toronto police to apologize for 1981 bathhouse raids," *Toronto Star*, Tuesday, June 21, 2016.
27. Thomas: Nicki: "Thirty years after the bathhouse raids," *Toronto Star*, Friday, February 4, 2011.
28. Isai, Vjosa: "Son of Bruce McArthur, the man charged with Gay Village murders, attends court in Oshawa on unrelated charges," *Toronto Star*, February 8, 2018.
29. "Online photos led to months of obscene telephone calls," *The Record*, June 11, 2014.

ABOUT THE AUTHOR

Alan R Warren is a Bestselling Author, the Producer, and lead host of the popular NBC Radioshow House of Mystery and Inside Writing, both heard on the 106.5 F.M. Los Angeles/102.3 F.M. Riverside/ 1050 A.M. Palm Springs/ 540 A.M. KYAH Salt Lake City/ 1150 A.M. KKNW Seattle/Tacoma and Phoenix.

His bestselling true crime books in Canada include *Beyond Suspicion: The True Story of Colonel Russell Williams*, which will be featured on CNN's *Lies, Crimes, & Videos* (Season 4), and *Murder Times Six: The True Story of the Wells Gray Park Murders*. In America, his bestsellers include *The Killing Game: Serial Killer Rodney Alcala*, which was featured on several television shows such as *Very Scary People* with Donny Walberg, Oxygen's *Mark of a Killer*, Reelz' *Killer Trophies*, and soon to be included in a four-part Sundance Channel documentary called *Death's Date*. His bestseller, *Doomsday Cults: The Devil's Hostages*, was featured on Vice's *Dark Side of the '90s*.

His latest series, *Killer Queens*, is a six-part book series covering murders that affect the Gay Community. So far, it includes Book 1 - Leopold & Loeb, Book 2 - Butcher of Hanover: Fritz Haarmann, Book 3 - Grindr Serial Killer: Stephen Port, and Book 4 - Bruce McArthur: Toronto Gay Killer.

ALSO BY ALAN R. WARREN

Killer Queens is a new series of historical fiction books based on true stories. Sources, such as police reports and newspaper articles, are examined to gather as many facts as possible surrounding each case. As with any work of fiction, some creative additions are made when telling these stories, usually within the conversations between the personalities involved. The various sources are the basis of these conversations and hopefully, make them come alive for the readers to help understand what was meant by those words.

LEOPOLD & LOEB: THE MURDER OF BOBBY FRANKS (KILLER QUEENS 1)

Book 1 of the series focuses on what has been called "The Crime of the Century" in 1920s United States. At the center of this murder case were Nathan Leopold Jr. and Richard Loeb – two wealthy University of Chicago students who, in May of 1924, kidnapped and murdered 14-year-old Bobby Franks.

With Leopold and Loeb, both

males, the dominance shifted from one to the other. Regardless of who held it, the result was the same. They were both very interested in crime and pushing the envelope for the next thrill. The vicious "thrill kill" of Bobby Franks was the bloody result of an intense and unhealthy co-dependent bond between the murdering duo.

As you read the exploration of the case in this book, ask yourself: Would these young men be as vulnerable to their manipulations today? If they couldn't have harnessed and used shame as a control tactic, would they have been as successful at recruiting a criminal counterpart? Finally, to what degree can we hold the prevalent homophobia of this era accountable as a force to bear on this tragedy?

BUTCHER OF HANOVER: FRITZ HAARMANN (KILLER QUEENS 2)

Book 2 of the series focuses on the serial killer of at least 27 young men and boys in Germany in the post-World War 1 era. At the center of this murder case were Fritz Haarmann and Hans Grans, who were lovers while committing these murders. It wasn't until the skulls and bones started washing ashore from the Leine River in Hanover that Germany realized they had a cold-blooded serial killer in their country.

Unlike Leopold and Loeb murder case covered in Book

1, where the dominance shifted from one to the other, Fritz Haarmann was the dominant partner in this case. He carried out each of the murders and dismemberment of the bodies himself, even though he claimed that Grans chose who was to be murdered in court.

As you read the exploration of the case in this book, ask yourself, did Haarmann murder each victim to keep his lover Hans Grans to stay with him? Did Grans decide who it was that was to be murdered? The evidence on this case will keep you on the edge of your seat, trying to determine who was really behind these gruesome murders.

GRINDR SERIAL KILLER: STEPHEN PORT (KILLER QUEENS 3)

While the previous two books of this series explored the lives and murders of LGBTQ people in the early twentieth century, Book 3 focuses on more modern times. It is based on the case of Stephen Port, a serial murderer in London, U.K., who was convicted of drugging, raping, and murdering four young men. He was also convicted of drugging and raping several other

men. His victims were found through a new type of gay sex parties called 'Party N Play' or 'Chemsex' parties that have become all the rage.

This case has stirred a much-needed education about the whole LGBTQ community. It resulted in a new awareness of the everyday dangers facing gay men. The impacts of this case were considerable. A formal inquest into the police investigation confirmed that police failings probably contributed to the tragic fate of many of Port's victims. Many changes in how the police investigate modern-day crimes followed. It has even inspired the making of a U.K.-based TV series, Four Lives.

This book contains numerous actual letters from serial killer Stephen Port. They offer the reader a great perspective on how he thinks. Astonishingly, Port fancied himself a nurse and even provided advice on how to stay safe while working in the sex trade. Did Stephen Port kill these men and possibly more? Or was he just an innocent man who got into a lifestyle of chemsex, and it was merely bad luck that at least four of his partners who participated in chemsex with him turned up dead?

MURDER TIMES SIX: THE TRUE STORY OF THE WELLS PARK MURDERS

"The author even had me (who conducted the interview) on the edge of my seat as I was turning the pages as "the Detective" was trying to unearth the unspeakable truth."

— SGT. MIKE EASTHAM R.C.M.P.

It was a crime unlike anything seen in British Columbia. The horror of the "Wells Gray Murders" almost forty years ago transcends decades.

On August 2, 1982, three generations of a family set out on a camping trip – Bob and Jackie Johnson, their two daughters, Janet, 13 and Karen, 11, and Jackie's parents, George and Edith Bentley. A month later, the Johnson family car was found off a mountainside logging road near Wells Gray Park completely burned out. In the back seat were the incinerated remains of four adults, and in the trunk were the two girls.

But this was not just your average mass murder. It was

much worse. Over time, some brutal details were revealed; however, most are still only known to the murderer, David Ennis (formerly Shearing). His crimes had far-reaching impacts on the family, community, and country. It still does today. Every time Shearing attempts freedom from the parole board, the grief is triggered as everyone is forced to relive the horrors once again.

Murder Times Six shines a spotlight on the crime that captured the attention of a nation, recounts the narrative of a complex police investigation, and discusses whether a convicted mass murderer should ever be allowed to leave the confines of an institution. Most importantly, it tells the story of one family forever changed.

JFK ASSASSINATION: THE HOUSE OF MYSTERY INTERVIEWS - VOLUME II

The House of Mystery Radio Show has been on the air for ten years, broadcasting in over a dozen cities in the U.S. It started as a way to interview guests knowledgeable in many of the world's mysteries involving crime, science, religion, history, paranormal, conspiracies, etc. The House of Mystery Interview series is a curated collection of interviews from the show. Each volume focuses on one of the mysteries, providing the background and reproducing the main points discussed in the interviews. There will be no

committed answer at the end, as the Interviews series does not attempt to solve the case. Instead, it provides the most compelling aspects of each theory held by different experts. This series is an excellent reference for researchers and a good overview for those unfamiliar with the case. Online links to the actual interviews are included.

Volume 2 of the Interview Series, "JFK Assassination," covers the unrivaled historical mystery of historical mysteries. The JFK assassination is the grandfather of all conspiracies in America and arguably where they all started. A highly popular President with movie star looks and charisma, effecting significant changes in society, was brutally cut down in his prime. The official story was that JFK was killed by a sole assassin, Lee Harvey Oswald. However, many conspiracy theorists believe in an assassination plot involving the FBI, CIA, U.S. military, VP LBJ, Cuba's Fidel Castro, Russia's KGB, the Mafia, or some combination of those entities.

The research and interviewing of the JFK assassination experts lasted for over six years. Arguments and counter-arguments from a diverse mix of bestselling authors make for some interesting discussions. And some of the authors interviewed are considered just as controversial as the mystery itself. Most authors focused on who they believe was responsible for the assassination. Others narrowed their focus on certain related aspects, such as the Zapruder film, Nix film, Garrison Tapes, etc. All information collected from each expert adds value to the overall mystery.

www.ingramcontent.com/pod-product-compliance
Lightning Source LLC
Chambersburg PA
CBHW060515100426
42743CB00009B/1326